"The impact of being a faculty member of color comes from simply being here. My presence enriches the educational experience of all students. Clearly, I provide an inviting environment in which students of color may come for support and mentoring. I have been pleasantly surprised by the number of majority students that have come to me for course, career, and life advice. Upon reflection, I have determined that by doing my best in the classroom, in research and in service to the university, I break down the perceived barriers that race presents and have replaced them with an access bridge for others in the university community to cross."

Dr. Nicole Thorne Jenkins, University of Kentucky

"I figured in the long run, I would be better off—not only economically, but because of the fact that you can make a difference in people's lives."

Dr. Francisco Roman, George Mason University

Living The Dream

A New Generation of Minority Business School Professors

The Dream Continues
Seventh Edition

The PhD Project

Foreword by
David A. Wilson
Past President and CEO
Graduate Management Admission Council

Introduction by
Bernard J. Milano
President, KPMG Foundation and The PhD Project

Canyon Mountain Publishing
New York, NY

Living The Dream: A New Generation of
Minority Business School Professors
Copyright © 2016 by The PhD Project and
Ned Steele Communications, Inc.

ISBN: 1-59196-401-6

First Printing: November 2003
Seventh Edition: September, 2016
Printed in the United States of America

The PhD Project
Montvale, NJ

Canyon Mountain Publishing,
New York, NY

TABLE OF CONTENTS

Foreword

Stay the Course

Robert E. Witt, Chancellor of the University of Alabama System, chaired the Graduate Management Admission Council® Board of Directors some years ago. Addressing the board, he once said, "It will probably be ten years before even a trickle of returns can possibly come from this investment in The PhD Project. And even then, the returns may be none, they may be slight, or they may be exceptional. But if we don't stay the course today, we will never know what might have been."

The creation of The PhD Project over twenty years ago was not a task for the faint-hearted. But, as the pages of this book so powerfully attest, staying the course—remaining committed to the ideal of greater diversity at the highest levels of higher education—has yielded rewards that are worth every dollar invested, every moment of anxiety, and every word of persuasion.

The faculty—the Ph.D.s—whose pictures and stories compose this book are the dividends returned on a substantial investment in intellectual capital. Most important, they are

2

pioneers and heroes. They made a bold decision about their lives and careers and subjected themselves to the slings and arrows of a doctoral program. They forged new paths and built new models of leadership. And today they stand in the classrooms of this country as role models, as mentors, and as evidence that nothing much happens without a dream and the tenacity to make it real.

But with a dream and with the continuing support of schools, faculty advisors, and benefactors, and with the intellectual and emotional commitment of a community that believes in your cause, dreams are only the first step into a new and better world.

This year marks the twenty-second year The PhD Project and the Graduate Management Admission Council have renewed their mutual commitment to an ideal vision of doctoral education. Twenty-two years, and for GMAC®, over $4.3 million. *Was it worth it?* you ask. The answer, so evident as you read the stories in this book, is a resounding *absolutely*.

To each of you whose story is told in this book, we stand in admiration. To those of you who are still in the throes of doctoral work, we are committed to supporting you in your studies and as you enter the ranks of the academy. As you stay the course, so will we.

David A. Wilson
Past President and Chief Executive Officer
Graduate Management Admission Council

Introduction

The KPMG Foundation is very proud to be one of the founders of The PhD Project along with Graduate Management Admission Council, AACSB International, and Citi Foundation. While our success in increasing the numbers of minority faculty and the qualitative impact on business education are documented, the personal connection we have with doctoral students and faculty, and in many cases their families, has been the most gratifying. The individuals whose stories are chronicled in this book, along with the hundreds that are not, are true heroes. Their struggle, effort, and energy to complete their doctoral studies are truly inspiring. They have put aside careers, uprooted their families, and incurred financial hardship to chase their dreams. In fulfilling those dreams, they are making a very positive difference in the education and preparation of all students with whom they come in contact.

This journey started in September 1993, with twelve persons meeting in St. Louis to explore how to increase the diversity of business school graduates. That meeting was

4

followed by several others, each time expanding the invitation list to enhance the input. The outcome of that process was a recognition that we had to attack the problem systemically. That led to a realization that there had to be a significant increase in the number of minority role models and mentors in the front of the classroom. Thus, The PhD Project was created.

The KPMG Foundation has administered The PhD Project since its inception and continues in this role today, even after The PhD Project became a separate 501©(3) in July 2005. In addition to the administration, we are the principal funder, having provided almost one-half of the $44 million invested to date.

We are proud of the roles we have played in making this program a remarkable success. We are grateful for the time, talent, and financial support we have received from so many corporations, professional, and academic organizations.

As further evidence of the success of the Project, academic organizations and individual colleges and universities provide about 30% of the current annual budget. This is a true partnership of corporations, foundations, and business higher education.

And, as the stories in this book demonstrate, we are making a considerable impact on higher education.

On the following pages, you will read about the journeys of The PhD Project participants who have defended their dissertations and are now on faculty at colleges and universities around the country. Their stories are inspiring, uplifting, encouraging, and most importantly—true. Enjoy the ride.

Bernard J. Milano
President, KPMG Foundation and The PhD Project

The Business School's perspective

An Exemplary Program

For more than two decades, The PhD Project has been a shining light in the ongoing effort to increase the representation of minorities on business school faculties. It has been a powerful, constant, and effective force in increasing diversity and excellence within the ranks of U.S. business schools.

Academe faces a new challenge today, and in the years ahead, as the number of Ph.D.s in management education continues to shrink relative to growing demand. This trend poses serious questions for all business schools. How, in such an environment, can higher education continue to provide the high-quality, scholarship-based teaching and research that makes academic business schools unique? In this context, The PhD Project's role has never been more vital.

Many people mistakenly think, at first glance, that The PhD Project is simply a meritorious program to attract more African-American, Hispanic-American, and Native Americans to management education. It is indeed this—and an innovative, successful approach at that. But it is more. The PhD Project is attracting people of extraordinary quality to the academic community. Their commitment, dedication, intellectual spark, and unique perspective of having worked in the corporate environment have already begun to greatly enrich management education, as you will see in these pages.

The PhD Project has been adept at identifying, attracting, and encouraging exceptional people who might not otherwise have chosen to become business professors. Not content with having achieved all this, The PhD Project has also created a forum, unlike any other in the country, in which business schools can meet and exchange ideas with this remarkable group of future professors.

AACSB is proud to have sponsored this program since its earliest days. We applaud The PhD Project model, which has contributed to management education in so many ways, including the production of doctorates in management education around the world. Doctoral faculty are the lifeline of academic business schools. The PhD Project continues to be one of the exemplary programs that sustain this lifeline, enhancing the fabric and context of management education.

John Fernandes
Past President and Chief Executive Officer AACSB International

The Business perspective

Reaching Our Goals

It all began in 1994 with just $5,000 from (then) Citigroup and $5,000 from the KPMG Foundation. A very small investment to make in something that is having such a huge impact today. We are grateful that at the time, our leadership had the foresight to see the value in this unique model. And, that we have been able to substantially increase our funding and maintain this commitment over the past twenty-two years.

The Citi Foundation is committed to enhancing economic opportunities for individuals and families, particularly those in need. We know that in today's global economy, economic empowerment is inextricably linked to obtaining a higher education. The PhD Project has made tremendous strides in increasing the number of minority professors in the classroom, thus providing role models to inspire future generations of minority students to obtain a college degree; the key to their own career success and financial freedom.

Like the people profiled in this book, Citi's commitment to diversity runs deep. Because we serve clients from every walk of life, every background and every origin, Citi's goal is to have its workforce reflect this same diversity at all levels. We seek to have an employee population that is similar in composition to the population of our local communities.

Our support of The PhD Project enables us to carry out our goal of a diverse workforce. We are proud to champion such a great organization.

I have the privilege of serving on The PhD Project's board of directors and bear witness to the astounding impact The Project is having—not only on higher education, but the business world as a whole.

Ana Duarte McCarthy
Global Workforce Diversity Consultant
Citigroup

The PhD Project

The PhD Project, a multi-million dollar diversity effort sponsored by some of the nation's largest companies, is assisting African-American, Hispanic-American, and Native American professionals to return to academia and become business professors.

The PhD Project was founded in 1994 with five objectives:

1. To increase the number of minority business school professors who will function as mentors and role models;
2. To influence more minorities to pursue business degrees/careers;
3. To increase the number of qualified minority applicants to fill critical positions in the business disciplines;
4. To improve the preparation of all students by allowing them to experience the richness of learning from a faculty with diverse backgrounds, and;
5. To reach the goal of a better prepared and more diversified workforce to service a diversified customer base.

The PhD Project, now a 501(c) (3) organization, has been responsible for the increase in the number of minority business professors from 294 in 1994 to 1,344 today. Further, 278 minorities are currently enrolled in doctoral programs, and will take a place at the front of the classroom over the next few years.

The PhD Project's Impact

The PhD Project conducted two surveys—one of business school deans and the other of undergraduate and graduate students at U.S. colleges and universities. They were created in an effort to gauge the impact minority professors are having on the recruitment and education of minority and non-minority students.

The survey of deans revealed that a majority (72%) of them have seen an increase in the percentage of minority staff compared to ten years ago. Also, more than half (55%) see an increase in minority applicants for faculty positions. Seven in ten (69%) of the deans report that students are better prepared for a career in business when they had a minority business professor or doctoral teaching assistant.

Other results from the dean's survey included:

❖ **73% of respondents said that minority professor and/or minority doctoral teaching assistants are having a positive impact on career mentoring of minority students.**
❖ **70% of respondents said that minority professor and/or minority doctoral teaching assistants are having a positive impact on attracting minority students.**
❖ **68% of respondents said that minority professor and/or minority doctoral teaching assistants are having a positive impact on the education of minority students.**

The survey of students (who were taking classes from a minority teacher at the time) revealed that minority professors are having an astonishing impact on the education of both minority and non-minority students. When asked, **92% of students believe that minority professors are positively impacting the education of** *minority students* **and 86% percent believe they are positively impacting the education of** *non-minority* **students.**

Other results from the student survey* include:

❖ **80% of all respondents feel their professors have an impact on their career decisions.**
❖ **77% of all respondents feel that students will be better prepared to work in a diverse business environment as a result of their having had a minority professor.**

The results reinforce The PhD Project's mission: The students polled feel minority professors are impacting positively on their education, hence preparing them for a more diversified workforce.

* The student and dean's surveys conducted by the Hodes Group, based in New York, on behalf of The PhD Project. For full survey results, visit www.phdproject.org.

How The PhD Project Works

The PhD Project uses a three-pronged approach to increasing the number of minority professors:

- It markets a career as a business professor to minorities.
- It gives prospective doctoral students the information they need to decide whether an academic career is right for them.
- It sponsors and administers peer-support organizations for minority business doctoral students. These Doctoral Students Associations—DSAs—have been critical to achieving a very high retention rate.

The PhD Project conducts a nationwide marketing campaign—identifying minorities willing to leave their corporate jobs, return to academia to earn a Ph.D., and become business professors. Top candidates are invited to a three-day conference, where they meet with current minority business professors and representatives from Ph.D. programs across the country. They get all the information they need to make the transition from business to academia. Airfare and lodging for the conference are paid by The PhD Project.

Once enrolled in a doctoral program, PhD Project participants are invited to join one of The PhD Project Doctoral Students Associations. These peer support groups help minority doctoral students stay in touch to break the isolation often felt by doctoral students.

- **Among the participants in The PhD Project, the completion rate of doctoral students is 90% as compared to the overall dropout rate of approximately 70% as reported by AACSB.**
- **Of the over one thousand who have earned their Ph.D. since we started, 98% are in higher education teaching positions compared to the norm of 67%, as reported by AACSB.**

Following the dream

The clock told him

Dr. Leyland Lucas
Morgan State University
Ph.D. Rutgers University, management

Cruising down the MBA track at Howard University, Leyland Lucas was startled when a professor pulled him aside and asked if he had ever considered an academic career. "I said, 'That's not where I want to be.'"

But a seed had been planted, and Lucas eventually found himself in an adjunct teaching spot after he had returned to full time work. "I started noticing that I was looking at the clock when I was at work, to make sure I'd be out on time for my class." Soon he realized that "when I got in the classroom, there was a natural connection for me that hadn't been there before in anything I did."

In hindsight, Professor Lucas believes that the teacher who first planted the seed at Howard saw in him "a discipline, and a desire not only to learn but to share my knowledge with others." The professor knew, before he did himself, how to channel those qualities into an ideal career choice.

Dr. Lucas's commitment to academic life was put to the test in the first year of his doctoral program. His original advisers told him bluntly that he "didn't have what it took to be a Ph.D.— and I should think about returning to the private sector."

"I used that as motivation," says Dr. Lucas, who transferred to Rutgers University and earned his degree with distinction. Now a professor at Morgan State University, he says, "I always tell my students to aim for the stars—if you fail, you'll end up in the clouds."

"I set very high standards for my students. The harder I push them, the more prepared they will be. A student came back and told me, 'Because of what you are and what you represent, you've made me a better person.'"

The dream continues...

Now a tenured Associate Professor, Dr. Lucas is also Director of the Ph.D. Program at Morgan State—and by his second year in that position, had admitted a PhD Project doctoral student. He serves on the Shenandoah University Entrepreneurship Program Advisory Board, and has taught overseas in Ghana and Guyana. His research into minority entrepreneurship and capital access, and various strategy topics, has netted more than ten publications. He has worked to enrich his school's honors program and expand international recruitment and global research, teaching, and study opportunities for his students.

Coach puts him in the game

Dr. Peter Johnson
University of Alabama, Tuscaloosa
Ph.D. Arizona State University, accounting

Some business professors chart their career progression painstakingly; for some the calling is a matter of destiny. Then there's Peter Johnson.

A CPA who had earlier adjunct-taught an occasional college class, Dr. Johnson was content with his career in public accounting. He was living in Salt Lake City, Utah. His job opened him to such enjoyable assignments as preparing tax returns each year for his old college basketball coach, back in Hawaii.

The coach's neighbor was the dean of the business school at Brigham Young University's Hawaii campus. Over the back fence one day, the dean made a plea to the former coach: an accounting professor had just resigned unexpectedly. Did the coach know of anyone who could step onto the court for the upcoming academic year? The coach replied that he did.

When Dr. Johnson received the call from the dean, he thought it was a practical joke. "I had no desire to be an academic," he said. "I was happy to be a CPA, and I didn't want to leave my firm."

But, he thought, one year as a professor in Hawaii might be fun—and it would enable his children to be near their grandmother, who lived there.

To his immense surprise, "I fell in love with teaching. It was hard work, but I loved the lifestyle. I realized I did know a few things about accounting that I could share."

Intrigued by the possibility of an academic career, Dr. Johnson traveled to New York to attend the annual conference of the American Accounting Association, the organization of accounting professors. Having seen the racial makeup of business school faculties, he was unprepared to meet a large group of African American professors and doctoral students. They were members of the PhD Project's Accounting Doctoral Students Association, and they embraced him as a future peer. Soon he was being introduced warmly to established professors and doctoral program administrators—the very people who hired new professors.

"I was still thinking about going back to public accounting when I went to that conference. I thought I was on a career path to be a partner. But it was a spiritual experience. I heard something tell me I had to get a Ph.D."

"Public accounting was exciting, but this was something that fit for me more," he elaborates. "I felt like this was my calling."

Dr. Johnson spent an additional two years of teaching and doing accounting work, getting his personal and financial houses in order. Then he made his move. With two children (two more would follow), the Johnsons' plan was for his wife to work and help support the family. Soon after they arrived at Arizona State, she became ill and could not work. The Johnsons cut expenses and took loans. Once she recovered, he jokes, "It was just the usual stress of coursework and comps."

The first African American doctoral student in any business department at Arizona State, Dr. Johnson is the first African American tenure track faculty at Brigham Young University, Provo Utah. "Just being in front of the classroom makes a difference," he says. "It gives students of this school a different perspective."

Looking back on his unexpected path, Dr. Johnson says, "I didn't have a very strong educational background or training. If I can do it, anyone can."

The dream continues…
Dr. Johnson conducts research into financial reporting, disclosure and valuation, and analysts' forecast revisions. He has published on these and other several accounting topics, and has presented at several conferences. He is a research workshop coordinator at his university, an Ernst and Young Fellow, and a KPMG Future Diversity Leader mentor.

At home

Dr. Beverly Venable
Columbus State University
Ph.D. University of Mississippi, marketing

"I think we all have a place where we feel we are where we belong, fully in our element," says new professor and former banker Beverly Venable. For Dr. Venable, despite a successful business career, banking was not that place.

"I always said, if I could do whatever I truly wanted, I would be a Ph.D. It was always here, on a college campus, that I felt at home. Whenever I was on vacation anywhere, if there was a college, I'd have to go see it."

While pursuing her MBA, she shared her dream with a professor who became a mentor. "He said, 'you should just do it, and I will help you do it.'"

She did, he did, and in just four years the onetime banker was reborn as Dr. Venable. The four years weren't always easy, but, she says, "every time I came to a rough spot, The PhD Project was there to provide support that was very powerful. It made the difference for me."

Dr. Venable has had her research published almost every year since beginning her studies.

The dream continues…

Dr. Venable is now Associate Professor of Marketing at Columbus State University, where her areas of interest are market research and international marketing. She has also researched and published on marketing in non-profit organizations. She is active in her community's Chamber of Commerce, and she has supervised students in a study of downtown business development opportunities in Columbus.

The power of diversity

Dr. Boyce Watkins
Ph.D. Ohio State University, finance

Dr. Boyce Watkins has no doubts about the powerful impact a diverse faculty can exert on students of color. He experienced it as an undergraduate, and it changed his life.

Studying at a predominantly white college with no minority faculty in his field, Dr. Watkins needed to see a faculty member whom he didn't know, on an administrative matter. Just as he approached the professor's office, an African-American man emerged.

"I was so accustomed to seeing only white faculty that I actually thought, 'Why's this guy coming out of the professor's office?'" he recalls.

The man, of course, was the professor. But Dr. Watkins was in for some more eye-opening.

The professor began to mentor the young man, and soon the two were friends, playing basketball together between serious discussion on academics and careers. When Dr. Watkins visited the professor's home one day, the second revelation took place.

"I looked around at this nice house and thought, 'Wow, where did he get the money for this?'"

Boyce Watkins had always relished learning and scholarly pursuits. Now he realized that not only could minorities become business professors, but they could also earn a respectable living at it. Before long, he began to pursue his own Ph.D. in business, with his mentor's backing.

The two men remain close friends to this day, and the experience reverberates clear through to the students Dr. Watkins works with every day.

As a professor and scholar, Dr. Watkins has found the job he always dreamed of. "A place where I could grow intellectually for the rest of my life, give back to the community, and earn prestige," he says. "To have my mother know that her son has accomplished something."

Deeply devoted to his research, Dr. Watkins still sets aside significant time for undergraduate students who show up at his door seeking guidance and direction. Frequently, though not always, they are minorities. Remembering his many lonely student days as the only minority in the classroom, and the professor who mentored him on the basketball court, Dr. Watkins gives his students all that he can. He even plays basketball with some.

"I am not here," he says, "to just blend in and be fat and happy."

Dr. Watkins is also a role model to any prospective doctoral student who does not have an MBA degree, or whose math background is sub par.

It is a common myth, as Dr. Watkins learned when he applied to doctoral programs, that the MBA is a prerequisite to the Ph.D. It is not necessary, as he found out. But a strong grounding in math is vital, especially in quantitative fields like finance. Dr. Watkins was not a math whiz, and he found himself falling far behind in his doctoral studies.

Rather than risk failure, he took a break from the program to brush up on his math skills.

He did this by returning to his undergraduate alma mater, enrolling in two Master's level programs in mathematics and statistics, and "studying day in and day out including Christmas and breaks" for three years. He emerged with twin Master's degrees.

"I was determined," he says simply. "Never before or since have I gone through such a long period where every day I would wake up thinking that I had to redeem myself."

Dr. Watkins returned to his doctoral studies, earning his degree at a different school than the one in which he had started.

In addition to being published, working with students, and developing research, he has since founded an association of Black Financial Economists, and written a book for college-bound African-American students.

His advice for those who plan to pursue a doctorate without an MBA: "Just remember, you still need credentials that demonstrate your potential, such as GPA or test scores."

The dream continues...
Dr. Watkins has become a nationally recognized advocate and expert on issues relating to race and society. He is a public speaker and consultant.

24

Eleventh hour stand-in

Dr. John Warren
University of Texas, San Antonio
Ph.D. University of Illinois, Chicago, information systems

Most people go to business networking events for the same reason: you never know what might happen.

All John Warren hoped to accomplish when he attended a Chicago area networking breakfast was to hand out a few business cards. But what happened to him there turned his life upside down, propelling him from entrepreneurship to academe.

A former executive at top pharmaceutical companies who went on to create, grow, and sell his own business at a tidy profit, Warren was leisurely contemplating his next career move when he strolled into the Chamber of Commerce event. He introduced himself by explaining that he wasn't sure what to do next, and, in the generous manner of a man with time on his hands, offered to help anyone present who might need business planning or counsel.

The first person to approach him afterwards was a part time professor at the local college, who wanted to know if he was familiar with a popular spreadsheet program. The man then made an astounding request: he confided that he was unexpectedly unable to meet a commitment to teach a class in that program scheduled to start very soon. "He felt obligated to find someone to fill in," Dr. Warren recalls. "He asked if I would please consider going in to talk to the program head about it."

The still happily unemployed entrepreneur visited the college the following day and heard the program head say, "I really need someone; will you do it?" It was a Thursday; the class would start on Monday. Dr. Warren said yes.

Five years later, "one thing building on another," Dr. Warren, who had never seriously contemplated teaching before, had cobbled together a pleasant existence as an itinerant adjunct professor, freelance corporate trainer, and consultant. But the travel was wearying, and he asked one of the colleges where he taught, "What would it take to get a full time position here?"

That was when John Warren realized he needed to add the title, "Dr." to his name. Ironically, one of his undergraduate students was first to tell him about The PhD Project, whose annual conference was about to take place a short drive from Dr. Warren's home. He applied and attended. "It literally changed my life," he says. "At the time I had three young children. My wife was not yet employed. Until then, I thought no one like me went into a doctoral program. But [there] I saw people who had families, people making sacrifices. I started thinking, maybe this is something I can do."

Driven by a love of teaching and mentoring students, Dr. Warren spent a year "getting my financial house in order" — stepping up consulting work to create a nest egg, refinancing his mortgage, clearing up debt. Then, reluctant to uproot his young family, he applied to and was accepted by the University of Illinois, Chicago.

Now a professor at University of Texas, San Antonio, Dr. Warren has had a paper accepted for publication, and is mentoring many students. "I like not only helping others gain knowledge," he says, "but being a presence in the class for those who might never have seen someone like themselves in front of a classroom."

26

The dream continues...

Dr. Warren stays away from Chamber of Commerce events and potential career-changing opportunities these days: "I love being a professor." He is developing a program for corporations, his college, and the local public schools to partner in attracting minority students to technology careers. Dr. Warren is faculty adviser to four student groups—ranging from the investment club to the gospel choir—as part of his ongoing search for minority undergraduates to recruit for business study. He has nine published articles, with more in the pipeline. His son has considered applying to a business Ph.D program.

Mom was fine with it

Dr. Ana Sierra Leonard
University of Cincinnati
Ph.D. University of Cincinnati, management

Working for some of the world's biggest and most prestigious corporations, Ana Leonard nonetheless had to roll with the punches every few years as mergers, acquisitions, contractions, and cutbacks would rear their heads.

Recharging herself at the beach during one uninvited bout of unemployment, she spotted a newspaper article about The PhD Project and the appeal of becoming a business professor.

"No more layoffs!" she told herself with a smile, and clipped the article. A few days later, still on the beach, she was assembling her application to The Project's conference.

Still, as a mother, she paused to consider the financial realities of enlisting for five years as a student.

Her response: research. She studied cost of living indices in the communities of the universities that interested her, and narrowed the choices to those where she could get by financially. "No New York City for me, and no place where I would have to pay $25,000 in private school tuition for my daughter," she says.

Dr. Leonard was also supporting her mother at the time, and it nearly derailed her path. After agonizing for weeks over how the choice would affect her mother, Dr. Leonard realized

28

that she had never sounded her out about the matter. "So I told her what it would mean, and she just said, 'Do it. I've been poor and unemployed before, I will find a job.' It had become a huge issue in my mind, but to her it was a non-issue."

Also, her husband had worked for the same bank for eighteen years, and had not been looking to make a change. "If I ever had stopped to make a list of all the 'cons' it would have been very hard. I just follow my heart, make a set of goals, and go for it."

Today, she says with pride, "I *am* a good teacher!" Unsolicited e-mails from former students, recounting how something they learned in class helped them in their job, arrive regularly. "I find that immensely rewarding. Everyone wants to have a purpose in life. It's very nice when you get that kind of feedback."

Dr. Leonard was the first from her doctoral program to win the graduate student teaching excellence award for both her business school and the entire university. Her mother, meanwhile, delights in showing off her daughter's new business card to friends as she boasts to them, "My daughter is a doctor."

The dream continues...

Dr. Leonard, now an associate professor of Management, has added on the role of Director of International Programs at the University of Cincinnati's Carl H. Lindner College of Business. She has published with her mentors and co-chairs, Dr. Ajay Mehra and Dr. Ralph Katerberg (who she met at The PhD Project conference in November, 1995), and is doing research, some of it presented at the Academy of Management, relating to the growing presence of minority doctoral students through The PhD Project (published in the Journal of Organizational Behavior). She has mentored minority undergraduates aiming for academic careers of their own. Her mom now boasts she has two doctor daughters: sister Mandy Ortiz earned a doctorate in marketing from the University of Alabama (Tuscaloosa) in June 2008.

Never give up

Dr. Frank Bryant
California State Polytechnic in Pomona
Ph.D. New Mexico State University, marketing

Taking stock of his life, Frank Bryant had to admit that things could hardly look worse.

Earning his MBA during the recession of the early 1990s, he returned to his economically depressed hometown, Buffalo, to a dormant job market. His brand new degree was good for nothing more than a series of low-level temporary jobs. Bryant, heeding a favorite professor's counsel, decided to become a business school professor himself.

He applied to five doctoral programs. He received five rejections. Where some people might have thrown their hands up in frustration and started scouring the want ads for burger-flipping jobs, Frank Bryant dug his heels in harder.

He ultimately landed a sales consulting position, and in his free time began reworking his game plan for entry to academe. But the months soon turned into years, and Bryant was not yet ready to brave the waters again.

Then, nearly five years after his ignoble return to Buffalo, Bryant lost his job and found himself in straits as dire as those before. This time, he hastened into action.

"I did research on which schools would be the best fit for me, and I applied all over again," he remembers.

He also signed up for a GMAT prep course, paying for it with his severance package and unemployment benefits. It boosted his scores by 70 points. New Mexico State University soon granted him admission.

Today, Dr. Frank Bryant is a highly-regarded marketing professor who implores his students, facing an economy just as challenging as the one that twice kept him out of work, to prepare by doing just what he did.

"I tell them, 'be willing to constantly educate and retrain yourself. Sometimes you have to make a career change, or go in a different direction, to make yourself more attractive. Go back to school instead of being stuck where you are.'"

How did the unemployed executive persevere in the face of such massive initial rejection of his chosen path? "I wasn't too happy in the corporate world, and so I made becoming a professor my sole goal," he says. "I didn't want to be a management type, and I didn't like sales—and if you're going up the ladder in corporate life, that's where you're headed."

The life of a professor, Dr. Bryant notes, "fits my personality. It is an opportunity to work and learn at the same time." Professor Bryant frequently writes job and graduate school recommendations for his students, and many of them have stayed in touch with him years after graduating.

Today, Dr. Bryant reflects on the initial trepidation about committing several years to the rigorous life of a doctoral student. "I just went for it," he says, "and didn't dwell on it. I knew that at the end of the day, it would be worth it."

The dream continues...

Dr. Bryant is currently Associate Professor at California State Polytechnic in Pomona. In 2008 he published an article he co-wrote on micro-culture markets in Journal of Immigrant and Refugee Services. In 2007 he was published in Journal of Global Business.

Hard choice, easy decision

Dr. Francisco Roman
George Mason University
Ph.D. University of Arizona, accounting

Francisco Roman had just earned his Master's degree in economics, and the future looked bright. But a tough choice loomed ahead for the young financial analyst: on one side of his desk sat two exciting job offers in trans-national companies.

Spread out on the desk's other side was a stack of Roman's application papers for doctorate study in business. Also occupying a corner of desk space as if to punctuate the magnitude of his choice: a snapshot of his wife, a student, and his young son—each seemingly asking in silence, "Can you support me?"

Tough choice, easy decision. Francisco Roman, despite a successful Fortune 500 career as a management accountant, had yearned ever since entering his Master's program to teach college. He pushed the job offers aside and plunged into a new life as a Ph.D. student. He is now Dr. Roman and relishing every day of it.

"I just thought the transition would be easiest to do it right then," he says. "Here was a chance to have an impact on people's lives, to share your knowledge with others, and contribute something positive to society."

During his Master's program, Dr. Roman had been invited to teach a class at the junior college where years earlier he had begun his own higher education. The experience ignited an urge in him to become a professor.

"The opportunity cost for me was very high, considering the two job offers I held," he says. "I figured in the long run, I would be better off. Not only economically, but because of the fact that you can make a difference in people's lives both by teaching and doing research."

Today Dr. Roman sees that the seemingly large financial tradeoff in his choice was actually an investment—the cost being his reduced income for the five years of doctoral studies. His strategies for coping included teaching during summers and off-hours, selecting a school that provided a stipend, and taking some loans. But now his compensation as an accounting professor will more than cover that cost within another three years or so. Meanwhile, he is already reaping psychic rewards.

"I get e-mails from many students who have gone on to graduate and get jobs. They tell me how they are now using the material we covered in class to help them at work. This is a good feeling for me. More than anything else," he says, "is the personal satisfaction I receive."

Dr. Roman has been honored for excellent teaching, and is working on several research topics. His advice to anyone considering a doctorate in business: "It is critical to find out if this is something you really, really want to do, because it is a huge commitment—not only financially, but because it will take time away from your family and friends."

"Yet," he adds, "there are so many rewards."

The dream continues…

The rewards of his career choice continue to amass for Dr. Roman, now at George Mason University. His first publication appeared in 2007 in the Journal of Accounting, Auditing, and Finance, and it was reported on by The Economist magazine. Additionally, he has published articles in the following journals: Accounting, Organizations, and Society, Journal of Financial Economics, Issues in Accounting Education, and the Journal of Management Accounting Research.

Never too late

Dr. Angelisa Gillyard
Ph.D. Ohio State University, logistics

Undergraduate math major Angelisa Gillyard came *this close* to landing a job in her chosen field after Graduation Day, and to never setting foot in either academia or the business world.

Completing the last semester of her senior year at Spelman College and preoccupied with applying to graduate programs in mathematics and pursuing corporate job interviews, she needed one elective course to round out her schedule.

She chose a business class, and it changed the direction of her life almost instantly.

"I got turned on for the first time to using analytical thinking in the real world," she recalls. "It all just clicked. I found I liked solving problems that were real, not mathematical, and being able to apply solutions."

So in the waning days of the academic year, she walked her application for MBA school across town to Georgia Tech, not even having taken the GMAT exam, making the final deadline for applying by one day. Assuming that it was all too late anyway, she accepted a job testing software code.

One week later Georgia Tech accepted her, provided that she take the GMAT and do well. She did, and that September the math major became an MBA student. But midway through her studies, she took an internship at a Fortune 500 company that almost convinced her she had made a colossal mistake: while continuing to be fascinated with business problems, she found herself less thrilled with the actual day-to-day life of a corporate manager.

Then, just as she was contemplating her next steps, the impulsive finger of fate intervened. The notion of earning a doctorate had long been percolating on a back burner for Dr. Gillyard, whose mother is a college professor. But she had never pursued it.

Angelisa's mother, attending a large charity organization conference full of strangers, encountered a woman she did not know. Unexpectedly, the woman started talking about The PhD Project and its program to help minority corporate executives become business professors.

Angelisa's mother hurried home to share the news with her daughter. Within a few short months, Angelisa was attending the annual PhD Project conference, where Ohio State recruited her aggressively and offered her a fellowship.

Professor Gillyard has already been a role model for many minority students who have told her she was the first African-American they ever saw in front of a classroom. Plunging energetically into research, she has several papers now in the pipeline awaiting publication.

The dream continues...

Dr. Gillyard served as Assistant Professor at three universities over several years, worked in business consulting and then returned to college teaching in a new role that enabled her to pursue her other passion, the performing arts. She has studied the career patterns of women in logistics, among other topics.

Catalyst

Dr. Patricia Martinez
Loyola Marymount University
Ph.D. University of California, Irvine, management

As a promising doctoral student on the job market, Patricia Martinez was seeking a home at a strong, Hispanic-serving college when she visited informally at the University of Texas, San Antonio. Interviewing with the head of the doctoral program there, she found herself being whisked, to her astonishment, into introductory meetings with the business school dean and the president of the university.

"It was like the CEO of a company taking a personal interest in the hiring of a middle manager," she says now, still amazed at the experience.

Dr. Martinez accepted a position at UTSA, a school where more than half of the students, but fewer than 15% of the faculty, are Hispanic. "On the first day in class, I saw the young Latina women just sitting there and smiling at the sight of me."

She has plunged headlong not only into teaching, but also into mentoring and helping students outside the classroom. "One student told me, 'All of my professors are wonderful, but there are just certain questions I feel more comfortable bringing to you.'"

"I'm on the other side of the desk now, and there are moments of recognizing the responsibility that I am making decisions that affect people's lives," says Dr. Martinez, who has already assumed responsibilities in her new employer's doctoral admissions process and diversity initiatives.

"I want to be a catalyst in people's lives," adds Dr. Martinez, who is already doing that and more.

The dream continues...

Now a tenure track professor at Loyola Marymount University in her native southern California, a family considerations-driven move that worked out happily, Dr. Martinez still experiences frequent reminders of the impact of minority faculty. Within her first year at LMU, she had two Hispanic undergraduates tell her that they were very happy to see here there, particularly because they had voiced their concern about the low representation of Hispanic faculty within the College of Business. Currently, the Hispanic faculty has increased to four. She also finds herself advising individuals who are associated with the PhD Project, whether its discussions with prospective minority applicants to doctoral programs or current doctoral students who are on the job market. She says, "The role that the PhD Project played in my decision to pursue the degree is so great, that I have made a commitment to talk to any current or prospective PhD Project student who seeks my advice. It's my responsibility to pay back the help I received along the way." Recently, she advised doctoral candidates on the job market, a Latino, Native American and African American, whom she worked with either as a doctoral faculty member or Management Doctoral Student Association advisor. Dr. Martinez still collaborates on research with former UTSA colleagues. She has published several papers and injects issues of diversity in HR management into her teaching and research. And it continues to happen...again this semester, two Latina students sitting in the first row of the classroom seem to be smiling at her a lot.

Camel boy

Dr. Yusuf Nur
Indiana University, Kokomo
Ph.D. Indiana University, management

No one has traveled a longer route to a Ph.D. than Yusuf Nur, born in Somalia into a family of nomadic, impoverished goat and camel tenders.

As a young boy, he was expected to grow up and take his place among the elders herding animals. Then, at age five, a difficult life turned even bleaker. Yusuf's father died unexpectedly.

An aunt who lived in a big city came to his rescue. She took him in, raised him, and saw to it that the boy received an education. "Otherwise," he says, "I would have been a camel herder—a camel boy."

Through his teens and into young adulthood, education drew Dr. Nur like a powerful magnet. Raising his nomadic roots to a global scale, he traveled to Russia to study, and ultimately came to the United States, where in 1986 he enrolled in an MBA program.

Marrying and deciding to remain in the US, Dr. Nur worked for non-profit organizations for several years. Then he grew intrigued by the entrepreneurial opportunities arising in newly democratized Russia. Enrolling in some courses at Indiana University to brush up on his Russian, he squeezed in a class in international business. The business professor soon asked the language student to be a teaching assistant in the business school. The offer included a scholarship. Dr. Nur accepted.

Then the professor urged Dr. Nur to switch fields and become a Ph.D. student in management. At the time, Indiana's doctoral program was admitting two out of forty applicants. Dr. Nur told the professor he didn't like his odds.

But the professor persisted. Further, Dr. Nur had to admit, Russia's transition to capitalism was not proceeding as smoothly and swiftly as he had hoped. Already successfully teaching three sections in his first semester as a T.A.—"The professor just thought it would be interesting for me to share my experiences in places I'd traveled"—he took the GMAT for the first time, applied formally to the doctoral program, and was hastily accepted.

"When I started teaching, I realized it was in me," he recalls. "The transition was very quick. I am a people person, and the best part of this job is relating with the students, helping them understand things, and sharing examples and experiences."

In addition to his classroom teaching, Dr. Nur volunteers in a mentoring program for African-American undergraduates on his campus—an experience he finds fascinating because, as an African, he had had little first-hand experience working with Black men and women who were minorities. He has also mentored new doctoral students in his department.

In lasting and humble recognition of the distance he has traveled, Dr. Nur honors his roots in the personal e-mail address he has chosen for himself: "Camelboy."

The dream continues...

Dr. Nur teaches courses in international business and strategic management. He has teaching experiences in both areas at the graduate and undergraduate levels. His research interests include strategic leadership, cultural aspects of international management, and entrepreneurship and globalization and their impacts on economic development. Dr. Nur has presented at numerous conferences, and his research has been published in four journals.

Postcard from nowhere

Dr. Pamela Carter
Dean of Business & Technology at Community
College of Philadelphia
Ph.D. Florida State University, information systems

 Graduation Day loomed at the University of Maryland business school, but unfortunately for new MBA Pamela Carter, employment did not.

With a brilliant track record in her studies, she had performed admirably in a co-op work engagement with the Federal Reserve Board, and was anticipating a permanent job offer at a respectable salary.

She had no Plan B.

The offer did arrive, but it fell far short of her expectations. She declined it. With Memorial Day approaching and no job prospects in sight, she turned to her local newspaper's classified ads.

In small print, she spotted an opening for an assistant professor to teach office systems technology at Northern Virginia Community College. She had never even thought about teaching college before—but, she reminisces, "It sounded like it could be fun, so I decided I would try for it."

The college, impressed with her credentials, hired her and put her to work. She proved to be a standout in her first year. But that was when state budget cuts struck the public college.

Dr. Carter, the new professor on the block, had no seniority and was first in line to be dismissed.

Then The PhD Project mailer dropped into her mailbox. It was two days before the conference application deadline when she read it.

That night, Dr. Carter stayed up until 3:00 a.m. completing the application. The next morning, she FedEx'd it to meet the deadline.

Meanwhile, her department chair was furiously maneuvering to save the job of his newest professor. Two senior faculty members decided to retire, clearing enough budget room for Dr. Carter to be retained. But having considered the broader possibilities, she declined with thanks and applied to doctoral programs.

"Sometimes," she says, "you're on a path that's meant to be. A postcard comes out of nowhere, you go to a conference, and things start happening."

Fate played a greater role than she had realized at first. Dr. Carter's strong first choice was Florida State University. One of the Maryland MBA professors she asked for a recommendation had, it turned out, been a visiting member of the business faculty at Florida State recently. When Florida State's committee read the recommendation from a former colleague, it gave Dr. Carter's application greater weight. She was accepted.

Dr. Carter and her husband, facing a significant cut in income, also had the bad luck to be selling their suburban Washington home during a dip in the real estate market. To make ends meet, they realized, it would be necessary to forego vacations and take out loans. "My five dollar jars of olives had to go too," she jokes. "When you are on a budget, you have to go without some of the little things that make life pleasurable."

How did she and her husband cope with the necessity of making those sacrifices? "We knew why we were doing it, and we knew it was temporary. We knew what the rewards would be later."

"In the Ph.D. process," Dr. Carter adds, "you learn what is really important. That's what gets you through."

The dream continues...
In January 2016, Dr. Carter became the Dean of Business &
Technology at Community College of Philadelphia.

A moment of clarity

Dr. Terry Esper
University of Arkansas
Ph.D University of Arkansas, marketing

Terry Esper, logistics manager for Hallmark Cards, ended one lengthy corporate conference day with the social ritual of joining a colleague for a post-session beer. He was totally unaware the relaxing moment was about to change his life.

"He asked me," Dr. Esper recalls, "what I would do if I had enough money and didn't have to work anymore."

"I answered that I'd be in a school, reading and learning and teaching, for the rest of my life. I said it as a joke, but at that point I felt an inner pull. I started feeling that my years in industry were not my calling—they were about preparing me for my calling.

"It was a moment of clarity for me. I realized I was meant to be an academic."

The thought germinated within Dr. Esper for several weeks after he returned home to Kansas City, and then surfaced unexpectedly as he arranged an educational program for a professional association he belonged to.

"I wanted to get a new professor from my MBA alma mater to come and speak, and I called her for what I thought would be a twenty-minute conversation about the event. It turned into two or three hours of talk about becoming a professor. Something just connected with me during that call."

By the end of the conversation, the Hallmark manager and the professor had decided that they wanted to work together, and she had agreed to advocate for his acceptance into the doctoral program. It was March, past the application deadline for the University of Arkansas business Ph.D. program, and Dr. Esper assumed they were talking about something eighteen months in the future.

But the professor told him there was a position open for the coming year if he wanted it. Dr. Esper's application was speedily reviewed and approved.

With the professor Dr. Lisa Williams serving as his mentor, Dr. Esper was presenting at a national conference in his first year. Supported in part by a federal grant and stipend, he finished his program in three years—with three publications and three conference proceedings to his credit. He is now on faculty at the University of Tennessee. His research area is inter-organizational collaboration and supply-chain management.

"I could have taught with just the MBA, Dr. Esper says, "but the Ph.D. is about knowledge creation versus knowledge processing and regurgitation. I enjoy the research that I do as a professor very much."

The dream continues…

Dr. Esper received the Chancellor's Award, one of his university's highest honors, for his efforts to mentor and increase the representation of minority undergraduates, and has been nominated for other prestigious awards. He served as associate director of a program that enables local corporate executives to interact with and form mentorships with undergraduates. He no longer listens, in after-work social settings or anywhere else, to suggestions that he might want to consider changing careers.

You mean more

Dr. Danny Lanier, Jr.
Elon University
Ph.D. University of Georgia, accounting

The mailings finally got to him. Danny Lanier, public accountant, had reached that point in life and career where he was starting to wonder where true fulfillment might lie. It was then that he began paying closer attention to The PhD Project mailers that seemed to be arriving a couple of times a year with predictable regularity.

"It was successful marketing by The PhD Project," he explains. "After being pelted with mail, I said, 'alright.'" He attended a PhD Project conference. "I came in thinking this might be what I wanted; I left knowing that it was."

At the conference, he recalls, "I saw people I had known from INROADS and other programs. I saw one of my college instructors, who didn't have a Ph.D. It made me see there were others with common interests here; maybe this isn't such a crazy idea."

The conference sessions, at which professors described their lives, marked a turning point for him. "It seemed there could be meaning to what you do. Someone on one panel said that when you leave a corporate job, they just put someone else in your spot, and they go on. But when you are in academe, you mean more."

His decision made, Dr. Lanier identified universities that offered programs matching his interests, and then successfully pursued scholarship opportunities once he was accepted by the University of Georgia. Today, he takes great delight not only in his formal responsibilities, but in guiding students onto career tracks. He has converted several students from "undecided" to accounting major. Some of them have gone on to work at top-level accounting firms. He continues to receive messages from them, updating their progress and thanking him for his earlier guidance.

"Seeing them go out and succeed, and then come back to thank me," Dr. Lanier says. "It's priceless."

The dream continues...

Assistant Professor of Accounting Lanier says, "One of my favorite aspects of my position is being able to have an impact on students. I recently received a thank-you letter from a former student, thanking me for encouraging her to major in accounting (at the time she took my course, she was a finance major) and for being a mentor. Although I am tough, students have regularly selected me to host a table at our annual School of Business awards banquets."

Is this for me?

Cross the ocean

Dr. María T. Cabán-García
University of South Florida, St. Petersburg
Ph.D. University of Missouri, Columbia, accounting

María Cabán-García, already a college professor, lacked three things in her life: the letters Ph.D. and all they stood for. To earn them, she uprooted her life and family, left her native home in Puerto Rico, and took on a challenge so daunting that she dared not to dwell on it too closely.

Dr. Cabán-García had initially begun teaching accounting part time at the University of Puerto Rico, Mayagüez, to bolster her income as an accountant and consultant. Before long, she was teaching full time. But she sensed something missing. Her husband was an engineering professor at another college, and some of the faculty there engaged in research. In her college, there was no ongoing research and there were no doctorally-qualified accounting professors. The urge to do research and stretch her intellectual capacity became harder to resist with each passing semester. But changing her life was not an easy step. There were no Ph.D. granting accounting programs in Puerto Rico, she had a widowed mother, and there was an engrained cultural mindset to tackle: "When you live on an island, you tend to be very regional—you don't want to 'cross the ocean.'"

On the other hand, the timing was right—her three children were now aged fourteen through twenty, and her husband was open to the possibility of finding a professorship on the mainland. After many long discussions and much thought, the family agreed to support Mom's decision.

"It was a big step for us all," she says. "We left the place where we were born and grew up. My kids left their friends, their school, their family and their culture."

Dr. Cabán-García's husband found a visiting professorship at the same university that accepted her for her doctoral studies, and the deal was clinched.

What seemed like a daring step turned out to be a logical evolution of the family's growth. Dr. Cabán-García firmly believes that having her doctorate provides "a chance to lead the path for others—to do research, to help others who might have the same ambitions." Her children adjusted well—so well that her daughter is now pursuing a Ph.D. also—but, following Dad's footsteps rather than Mom's—in engineering.

"I look at where I was before and where I am now, and I see it has opened a whole new perspective," Dr. Cabán-García says. "In every way, I have moved forward."

Students—especially Hispanic Americans—flock to Dr. Cabán-García for career advice. When prospective doctoral students ask her about becoming a professor, she tells them how to know if it is the right move for them. "Practitioners have to be current in their profession. Academicians have to be a little bit ahead. You need a sense of vision. This is for people who are not afraid to change, or to adjust to change."

In other words, for people who can see the rewards of "crossing the ocean."

The dream continues...

True to her plan, Dr. Cabán-García is actively conducting research, especially into areas relating to international accounting, with several papers nearing publication. She teaches intermediate and advanced financial accounting while serving on several faculty committees and continuing to mentor students and provide career advice. Students find her especially helpful in providing perspectives on the choice between a career in public or private accounting.

Introvert or extrovert?

Dr. Michael Kimbrough
University of Maryland, College Park
Ph.D. Indiana University, accounting

At first the idea of Michael Kimbrough, rising star at a leading accounting firm, becoming a business school professor seemed just about half right to him.

Conducting research and delving into analyses of business issues had always appealed to him, but opportunities to do so in the deadline-delineated life of corporate client service were limited.

Still, as he considered a possible career switch to academia, Kimbrough hesitated. He had always thought of professors as extroverts—larger-than-life theatrical performers enthralling students with their dynamic presentation style. And Michael Kimbrough thought of himself as the less outgoing sort.

Then Kimbrough did his own research and dug deeper. As he reflected, he saw that "different types and styles work in a classroom." Moreover, he found the traits needed for the self-driven dynamics of earning a doctorate and in performing academic research as a professor, matched his own contemplative temperament ideally.

"I realized that being a professor requires you to call on skills and traits I did have," says Dr. Kimbrough.

In becoming a professor, Dr. Kimbrough has found the opportunity to embrace dual sources of satisfaction—the intense yet different kinds of personal rewards he attains by teaching and working with others, and by conducting and publishing research in his own name on the topics that most intrigue him.

"Being in the classroom," he explains, "is all about the students, and making sure they are 'getting it.' Research gives me the satisfaction of doing something that is purely my effort, my ideas, and my direction."

Dr. Kimbrough received five job offers after completing his doctoral studies, and he has published two articles, with others in the pipeline. Despite his early successes, he might not have become a professor had it not been for a role model who worked down the hall from him in the accounting firm.

"I was at that stage in my career where it was time to think about how to best leverage my experience for the next stage of my career. Now that I knew that life, did I want to invest in it for the long haul?"

As those thoughts turned over in his mind, office colleague Nicole Thorne Jenkins was attending The PhD Project's annual conference and starting out on the road that would eventually lead her to a professorship at Washington University. She shared her plans with Kimbrough, and he immediately felt it resonate within.

After exploring and resolving his "extrovert-introvert" preconceptions, he followed down the same path, attending the following year's PhD Project conference. The decision came at that critical early-career juncture "where you think the path of your life has been set." But after attending the conference, he recalls, "it was as if I was eighteen again, where your life feels like it is wide open before you."

Dr. Kimbrough also had to overcome his initial assumptions that the competitive nature of doctoral program admissions significantly limited the number of schools to which he should apply. At the conference, academics looked at his background and, based on his credentials, persuaded him to apply to a more ambitious set of schools than he might have initially.

The dream continues…

Dr. Kimbrough taught at Harvard and now is at the University of Maryland, College Park. He has published extensively, in several journals, as he continues to develop both the research and teaching aspects of his position. Teaching an advanced MBA course has enabled him to integrate his research interests into the classroom through cases he writes specifically for the class.

Learning curve

Dr. Laura Francis-Gladney
State University of New York, Institute of
Technology
Ph.D. Southern Illinois University, accounting

As a hopeful would-be doctoral student, Laura Francis-Gladney knew— well, not very much—about earning a Ph.D. or becoming a business professor when she first applied to a doctoral program.

In a seventeen-year government career in the New York City Controller's office, she had been frequently called on to conduct training sessions. She had liked it enough to conclude she was meant to be a college teacher. The one thing she knew was that if she wanted to enjoy job security and respect, she needed a Ph.D.

Beyond that, she admits with a smile today, "I didn't have a real clue."

When a local business school dean told her that the business Ph.D was a research degree, it was news to her. "I said 'sure, whatever.' I didn't know what that meant. It just went over my head—I thought I'd figure it out and do whatever I had to do."

The next thing Dr. Francis-Gladney didn't know about were the realities of doctoral program admissions. "The first time, I treated it like undergraduate school. I applied to just one school—I was an alum there, so I assumed they would take me."

To her surprise, her alma mater rejected her. At first Dr. Francis-Gladney concluded that she was not meant to be a professor. Soon after that, she saw an ad for The PhD Project and attended its next conference.

When the following year's admissions cycle came around, Dr. Francis-Gladney was considerably better prepared. She applied to eleven schools and chose to attend the first one to accept her with an offer of financial assistance—Southern Illinois University, whose representatives she first met at The PhD Project conference. Ten years out of MBA school, among the program's older students, and feeling "a little bit intimidated," she moved from New York to Southern Illinois, where she excelled. As a teaching assistant, she frequently assisted struggling and insecure students.

Laughing at her early naiveté, Dr. Francis-Gladney today serves on the faculty of SUNY Institute of Technology. Finding a comfortable balance between doing research and teaching, she reports that the appreciative notes and positive feedback she receives from her students are the most rewarding aspects of her new life.

The dream continues...

Naiveté long gone and balance attained, Dr. Francis-Gladney has studied and published on such diverse issues as nurse unionization and hospital care quality, utility industry mergers, and budgetary decision-making. She sponsors her university's Accounting Club, and through it participates in a program that helps students and low-income community people prepare their tax returns. "These activities are very rewarding," she says. In a new role, she counsels graduate students as program coordinator for the university's MS in Accounting program. "I continue to really enjoy working with and helping my students," she says.

"I'll get involved in your life"

Dr. Sammie Robinson
Houston Baptist University
Ph.D. University of Kansas, management

Sammie Robinson was a child of the 1950s. "I come from a background," she explains, "where the most optimistic dream was that I would attend a small Black college and maybe become a teacher."

But business appealed to the young woman, and although she did attend college, "it was a vocational experience." After graduating she worked as an accountant for several years in other states until, by now divorced and raising a small child alone, "I went home to Texas, where my intent was to go to the local phone company and get a position I could stay in until I retired.

"I worked there for twelve years. I made nice money, but I was a captive. I didn't like the job. So I decided that an MBA might make it easier to find a job I enjoyed more, with better pay.

"During my second trimester at Southern Methodist University, I took a course in Organizational Behavior and my eyes just opened. I started paying attention to what the professors were doing, and their lifestyle. I said, 'I want to do this.'

"I went to all my professors and asked them about their lives. I cold-called the few African-American professors I managed to learn existed.

"I gave up my house and my car, and I entered a whole new world after age forty. I had always been so vocationally- and practically-oriented. There were so many things I didn't know. Publishing, research methodology—I didn't understand anything about a research career. This whole idea of living a life of the mind—it's a concept that I am still coming to terms with."

Dr. Robinson believes her "mission" is to serve as a role model and mentor for minority students in predominantly white universities. "People who are somehow marginalized or disenfranchised gravitate to me. I will get involved in your life."

Her involvement has often been extraordinary. "There have been students whom people said were worthless, but if I see something in them, I'm willing to give them a second chance."

"One young woman was about to flunk out, but I said, 'I will give you a chance to take the class over without having to fail it first. Your end of the bargain is that you must meet with me once a week.' She earned a 4.0 that semester and she graduated."

As a doctoral student, Dr. Robinson won top honors for dissertation research and a best teaching assistant award. "I save every e-mail I get from a student thanking me. They see the value of what I've given them a year to two years out. When a student tells me I made a difference, that's it for me!"

In 2003, Dr. Robinson attended an academic conference at which she again encountered Dr. Lynn Isabella, the professor who had first inspired her as a student at SMU. "It was a real pleasure to thank her in person for writing letters of recommendation, and most importantly, to report that I finished my doctoral program," says Dr. Robinson.

57

The dream continues...

Dr. Robinson, now an Assistant Professor at Houston Baptist University, continues to take seriously her multiple roles as researcher, teacher, mentor, and role model. She has developed a prolific research stream on African-American woman entrepreneurs with PhD Project professors Dr. Laquita Blockson and Dr. Jeffrey Robinson, and developed an entrepreneurship studies program at her previous university, Prairie View (TX) A&T University. Having turned fifty the year she earned her doctorate, she says, "I am rejuvenated. I am where I am supposed to be." When her profile was posted on The PhD Project web site, it inspired one reader to contact her, initiate a mentoring relationship, and apply for and enter a doctoral program, where she is currently studying.

58

Something that lasts

Dr. Millicent Nelson
Middle Tennessee State University
Ph.D. Oklahoma State University, management

Millicent Nelson, born to a family full of academics and students, recalls that "teaching was a gift from God to me; I was always the one teaching people how to do things." But she restricted her instructing to the corporate world, where "I was having a great time" in seventeen years of frequent travel, promotions, and excitement in the field of telecommunications.

By the time endless corporate restructurings led to increasingly onerous work requirements and irresistible severance offers, she was ready to turn to her calling. But the most common reaction she received when sharing her plans with friends was, "But you're too old!"

"I told them if I was blessed, I'd be getting older anyway. So I might as well get old doing something I like."

Accepted into a doctoral program, she soon recognized that she had made the right choice. "When you are doing research and teaching, you are contributing to something that's bigger than you—something that's going to last."

A student in one of her classes often sat silently through each session, and "that was unacceptable to me, so I would call on him, and get him involved. After graduation he came to see me, and he told me he had lived on a farm all his life, and would be going back to work on it after graduation."

After a year on the farm, the student confided that he yearned to study for an MBA. Dr. Nelson walked him through the process, wrote him a recommendation letter, and because she knew the head of the program to which the young man was applying, introduced him personally. He is now an MBA student, planning to work in corporate America, and eventually become an entrepreneur, after receiving his degree. "Young people are the future leaders of our country, and as a professor you have the chance to influence them," she says. "That is powerful."

The dream continues...

Now a tenured Associate Professor at Middle Tennessee State University, Dr. Nelson is the incoming President of Management Faculty of Color Association (MFCA) and she served as co-Program Chair for the 2011 MFCA Conference. At the 2011 Academy of Management Conference, she coordinated a professional development workshop on "Managing the Tenure Process" and facilitated a panel symposium on "Academia as a 2nd Career from the Perspectives of Minority Faculty". She was the recipient of Distinguished Research Awards at the 2007 and 2008 Allied Academies International Conference. She has received two research grants from her university and has publications in conference proceedings and academic journals. She serves as coordinator and advisor for the Health Care Management Graduate Certificate Program at Middle Tennessee State, and was program co-chair of an International Diversity Conference there. Dr. Nelson is mentoring another graduate student who is having difficulty being accepted into the MBA program due to a marginal GPA and low GMAT score. She believes this student is capable of earning his MBA and becoming an outstanding employee so she is working with him to realize his potential.

Urban entrepreneur to academic

Dr. Jeff Brice, Jr.
Texas Southern University
Ph.D. Mississippi State University, management

In a career that started on the streets and has now turned to academia, Jeff Brice, Jr. has run his own film production company, headed a construction business, and worked on job-development with ex-convicts and welfare mothers. As an affordable housing developer, he recalls, "We'd go into drug-infested properties, kick out the dealers, and then get grants to get the buildings rehabbed."

The rough side of life was all-too-familiar territory to Jeff Brice as a young man. After a difficult childhood, he enrolled as an undergraduate at Tuskegee University. What his classmates and professors did not know was that he was homeless.

For more than two years as a student, Jeff Brice lived in a graveyard. Then he landed a job in a campus dormitory—it provided room and board. Pursuing an entrepreneurial road upon graduating, Dr. Brice became a music video producer "without even knowing what a producer was. I had no experience in films, but I found out that you could put a crew together for $25,000, make a video in two weeks, and get $100,000 for it. I saw an opportunity and I took it." A thriving business in creating videos for eighties-era rock groups ensued. But he moved on to other fields, because "I got tired of it.... I only do things that interest me."

Eventually, what interested him was studying business at the graduate level. That in turn sparked the young entrepreneur's interest in teaching college.

"Everything in the MBA program was corporate. My expertise was how to get access to capital from different sources, like grants. I thought I could bring to the classroom a more realistic view of how to build a business. My contribution could be to provide a more practical application of things."

The dream continues...

Dr. Brice is now a tenured Associate Professor and Chair of the Department of Business Administration at Texas Southern University. He manages the faculty (graduate and undergraduate) and degree programs in the areas of Business Administration, Management, Marketing, Management Sciences, and Management Information Systems. Several of his former students are now successful entrepreneurs, and he himself is still one, living by the credo, "If you can't do it, then you certainly shouldn't be teaching it!" He developed the curriculum for his university's interdisciplinary entrepreneurship program, and while at Hofstra University, was solely responsible for creating and teaching courses for that university's Bachelor's program in entrepreneurship. It went on to be recognized as one of the top fifty regional programs and one of the top one hundred programs in the U.S. by Entrepreneur Magazine. Dr. Brice has earned four consecutive distinguished research awards and he has published numerous articles.

62

A waiting room epiphany

Dr. Aberdeen Leila Borders
Kennesaw State University
Ph.D. Georgia State University, marketing

Five kids call Leila Borders "Grandma." Hundreds of young adults now call her "Professor."

In a quarter-century corporate career, Leila Borders had never entertained a thought of teaching until she sat in a doctor's waiting room one day in 1996, eyeing an article on a PhD Project participant. It was as if a light went on. "Something said, 'this is for you,'" she remembers.

A nurse fretted at the sight of the doctor's next patient dropping herself onto the examining table, still clutching a magazine and never lifting her eyes from its pages. "I asked her, 'What issue is this? I have to buy it.' She said, 'Just take it. I'd hate to separate you from it.'"

Two obstacles loomed in Leila Borders's path. She dispensed with both quickly.

One was perception over age—she was a young grandma, but a grandmother nonetheless. "I never thought I couldn't do it, but I wondered would I have the stamina? Finally my husband told me, 'You're spending more time thinking about this than you will spend doing it. Go ahead, and I'll support you. We'll work out the issues.'"

In addition, at the time, she was engaged in more than forty community, church, and social activities. Some had to go. Targeting some of her cherished pastimes for elimination was painful but necessary.

Dr. Borders soon made her midlife career shift. Age was never an issue once she returned to the classroom, although "I often played the role of Mama" with some of her fellow doctoral students.

She started as an assistant professor at the University of New Orleans (UNO). Most of that school's students remained in their hometown upon graduating and never worked in a corporation, although Dr. Borders is convinced many of them had the skills and mindset to succeed in the business world.

So, even as she taught a "principles of selling" course, Dr. Borders introduced her students to corporate life and showed them how to sell themselves to employers. Teaching undergraduate juniors, she realized that two-thirds of them had never written a resume. "All semester, I work with my students on their resumes. At the beginning, I ask, who doesn't have a resume, who isn't satisfied with theirs? Everyone raises his or her hands. I have them send me their resumes, and throughout the semester, we work on revising their resumes and preparing cover letters, as well as other career development activities such as mock interviews. I always tell them, 'Remember, you are selling yourself.' I have helped numerous students get jobs in this manner."

The students' first assignment generally is to prepare a resume and cover letter tailored to an actual job opening they see advertised. She then works with them throughout the year—investing more than one hundred hours of her time—to polish and perfect their resumes. "I see their self-esteem and confidence building by leaps and bounds as they become more assertive," she reports.

Dr. Borders touches many other corners of her students' lives. She has created an elaborate system to exchange notes and messages with each student throughout the semester. Using this channel, she has helped undergraduates successfully tackle a whole spectrum of challenges ranging from the academic to the personal.

64

The investment paid off for Dr. Borders the day she heard a former student tell a friend, "Listen to her—she is how I got my job."

In 2006 while at UNO, with the assistance of a Louisiana Board of Regents grant, Dr. Borders built and equipped a sales behavioral lab for students to develop their selling skills. Dr. Borders became UNO's first faculty coach to take students to compete in the National Collegiate Sales Competition (NCSC). The NCSC hosts the top collegiate sales talent and sales faculty from the most elite University Sales Programs in North America. Upcoming sales graduates are provided a venue for sharpening their sales skills in a highly competitive environment and networking with their peers and sales faculty from across the United States.

The dream continues...
Dr. Borders moved in 2008 to Kennesaw State University near Atlanta, GA as an Associate Professor where she additionally serves as an assistant director in the Center for Professional Selling, which hosts the NCSC. Dr. Borders has been published on numerous topics, including a social marketing perspective on the aftermath of Hurricane Katrina. Since her move to Kennesaw State University in 2008, she has been promoted to Full Professor and continues to mentor students extensively, and train, coach, and prepare them for employment interviews and professional selling careers.

Banking on a new career

Dr. Patricia Hewlin
McGill University (Montreal)
Ph.D. New York University, management

As a retail branch manager and vice president for one of the world's premier banking companies, Patricia Hewlin often found herself at the front of a training classroom, instructing employees in job skills. Before long, this rising corporate star realized that teaching, even more than banking, was her calling.

Fortunately, her employer knew just what to do. Citigroup—a founding sponsor of The PhD Project—encouraged and helped her to pursue a new career in academia, though it meant losing a prized employee.

"I was enjoying not only training my employees, but also watching them grow from level to level," says Dr. Hewlin. "I loved seeing the results, and I became interested in how employees get motivated to advance. Now I was more interested in diagnosing employee issues that had long-term implications for the corporation than fully devoting myself to short-term solutions, both of which are important to effective business management."

The successful banker discovered that "I was asking the kinds of questions that scholars had, and I was enjoying it."

"Companies understand that research and understanding lead to increased revenues, but in a fast-paced environment the emphasis is always on making the numbers."

Rather than dream or despair, Patricia Hewlin reached out. Aware that her company sponsored The PhD Project, she contacted a Citigroup executive familiar with the program who could tell her more. Within a year, she was accepted by a top university's Ph.D. program.

Today, Professor Hewlin is "doing exactly what I wanted to do." Students immediately sit up and pay close attention when their professor reveals her corporate background, and she draws on it frequently in her research and teaching. Students approach her for advice on careers and graduate study in banking, and she has guided several of them onto the path.

And, whenever Dr. Hewlin senses a potential match, she introduces her students to executives at her former employer— setting the stage for the day when Citigroup starts to recoup, several times over, the investment it made when it encouraged the rising young banker to leave the ranks and become a professor.

The dream continues...

Dr. Hewlin's research centers on the ways organization members express and suppress aspects of their identity, such as personal values and beliefs at work. Her research also spans to gaining insight on how members make sense of and cope with organizational value breaches in mega-churches and other values-driven organizations. Dr. Hewlin is an award winning scholar. She has several publications and has presented at numerous conferences in the US and abroad. Dr. Hewlin has been quoted in several print media, was featured in Black Enterprise magazine, and has appeared on BET News. She enjoys mentoring doctoral students and participates frequently in the Management Doctoral Student Association's annual conference. Her former employer, Citigroup, continues in its role as a founding sponsor of The PhD Project.

"Should" vs. "want"

Dr. Michael McMillan, CFA/CIC/CPA
CFA Institute
Johns Hopkins University (2002-2008)
Ph.D. George Washington University, accounting

 On New Year's Eve in 1988, Michael McMillan made a resolution to become a professor. Fourteen years later, that resolution became a reality. He is now called Dr. McMillan.

When Dr. McMillan was working in the corporate arena, he would find himself talking to friends and family about his long-distance teaching courses more than his corporate job. "All of my friends were in corporate jobs, so I thought I was supposed to be, too. I was doing what I thought I *should* do, not what I *wanted* to do," he says. So, in 1994, he started his doctoral process.

In 1995, a friend at school told him about The PhD Project. It sounded like just what he needed to get himself through. He attended the Accounting Doctoral Students Association, "and my life was changed forever."

"I always teach my students to finish what they start—and I lived up to my own creed. It took me seven long years, but I did it! And it's thanks to the support, friendships, and mentoring I got from The PhD Project," Dr. McMillan says.

The dream continues...

Dr. McMillan added "CPA" to his credentials in 2006 and continues to draw on his corporate experience in teaching accounting and finance, and in conducting research. When he was seeking a faculty position, many deans had told him he would have to choose between the two disciplines, but Johns Hopkins allowed him to pursue both. After six and half very satisfying and fulfilling years at Johns Hopkins' Carey School of Business, Dr McMillan joined CFA Institute in 2008. "I had been a volunteer for CFA Institute since 1996, first as a grader of the CFA examinations and then as a member of their Council of Examiners. Therefore, working for them full-time was like joining a family business. As the Director of Ethics and Professional Standards, I have the opportunity to use both my academic and professional skills and experiences. I provide ethics training all over the world to financial institutions, investments professionals, and our Program Partner universities. In addition, I have developed an online ethics course and have written a number of articles on ethical issues in the investment management field. Equally as important, I also participate in the Institute's diversity outreach efforts and we are ardent supporters of The PhD Project."

Programmed to succeed

Dr. Amanuel Tekleab
Wayne State University
Ph.D. University of Maryland, management

From high school days in his native Ethiopia on, Amanuel Tekleab yearned to become a professor. Spurred by parents who lacked formal schooling but placed great value on education, he set out after his dream. The path led to seven years of teaching business in his homeland, and then to the United States, where he entered the MBA program at Clemson University.

Midway through it, he learned that an MBA is not required for a doctoral degree in business. He swiftly enrolled as a Ph.D. student at the University of Maryland.

But despite nearly a decade in academe, Dr. Tekleab quickly realized he faced an obstacle—the perception of some others that, as an international student, he wasn't "good enough."

"I had to prove to a few faculty that I could do it, that I was equal at the least to the others," he recalls. "And I had to prove to myself that I could do research and complete a doctoral program."

To establish himself firmly, Dr. Tekleab set out a three-part strategy. He programmed himself to succeed by programming his time carefully and intricately. He found a mentor. And he worked very hard.

"I would work every day from 6 a.m. until midnight, and at the start of each semester, I would program my entire week by the hour," he explains.

"I would start with my class schedule, and then schedule in every hour—for research, writing, reading, and team projects. When I woke up in the morning, I knew exactly what I was going to do."

Dr. Tekleab wisely fit in time to start working with his department chair, Susan Taylor, who soon became his mentor. "I owe her a lot; she is almost like my mother," says Dr. Tekleab.

Dr. Tekleab has been published in the Journal of Organizational Behavior, and his first paper as a doctoral student won honors from the Academy of Management. But the most rewarding aspect of his new career, having learned "that people believed in me," is to believe in his students.

"I got all the support I needed when I was studying, whether for a research problem or a personal problem, and I am happy to transport this to my own students. There is nothing like seeing them gain something from what you teach, and then to see them graduate."

The dream continues…

Hard work continues to pay off for Dr. Tekleab, now an associate professor with tenure at Wayne State University in Michigan. He won a university-wide research award for junior faculty, carrying a research grant from his university for 2007- 08. He has had nine articles and a book chapter published, with an equal number in the pipeline, and presented or co-presented at two dozen conferences. He served on a doctoral dissertation committee in 2008. He serves on his school's research committee and Ph. D. program advisory committee.

A well-timed invitation

Dr. Dan Stewart
Gonzaga University
Ph.D. Stanford University, management

Dan Stewart, back in his undergraduate days, paid more attention to his professors than did most of his classmates. He was sizing them up as potential role models.

"I liked watching my professors, and I held them in high esteem," he says. "I thought that being up there and doing that was something I'd enjoy. But not having anyone in my family who had done it, I didn't know how."

It was 1991, and in one of those not-so-accidental coincidences, Stewart received an invitation to the Minority Summer Institute—a program that was then introducing minorities to a career in teaching business in college. "An administrator told me why I got it—I was studying business, had gotten good grades, and was involved in leadership activities."

He enrolled, immersed himself, and swiftly sold himself on becoming a professor. First on his agenda, however, was a four-year commitment to the military.

Fast-forward a decade, and Dan Stewart became Professor Stewart at Washington State University, having earned his doctorate at Stanford after completing Army service.

After concentrating heavily on research in his Ph.D. program, he teaches three classes each year. "I'm trying to become a good teacher," Dr. Stewart says. "I hope I can influence a few of my students to go for their Ph.D."

The dream continues...

Dr. Stewart is now a Full Professor of Management at Gonzaga University. He has published five articles on topics as diverse as Native American entrepreneurship and social status in an open source software community. He shares his experience by serving on the board of trustees of Spokane Tribal College, a Native American college, and he takes great pride in "working a new stream of research dedicated to understanding Native American entrepreneurship."

Sacrifice… or investment?

To MBA or not to MBA?

Dr. Angela Andrews
Indiana University-Purdue University
Ph.D. Michigan State University, accounting

For Angela Andrews changing jobs in the corporate world had become a depressing routine. "You're in a different cubicle, but it's the same job."

Despite a string of successful stints in financial accounting at top corporations, Dr. Andrews had never landed in the niche that felt just right. "I couldn't find the job that fit," she says.

As she was contemplating yet another job change, her mother—a former college secretary—called to tell her about a mailing she had received from a program called The PhD Project.

"That flyer changed my life," Dr. Andrews says. "When I read it, I thought, this may be what I've been looking for."

The PhD Project conference was a few weeks away, and she attended. "When it was over," she remembers, "I had tears in my eyes. I said, 'This is what I'm doing.'"

Dr. Andrews had never earned an MBA, and while she knew the master's degree was not required for doctoral studies, she wanted it nonetheless. Earning it, she determined, would shore up her strengths in accounting, and present an opportunity to score the stellar grades that had eluded her as an undergraduate in engineering.

But two years of full time study with five more years in a doctoral program piled on top was not a realistic option. She would have to continue working while pursuing the MBA. Over the next few years, she would slip into her cubicle at the office before dawn nearly every day, daily morning caffeine fix in hand, so she could leave early enough to attend evening classes. At home, she would study until 11:00 pm or midnight, fall into bed, and arise in the dark to do it all over again. Weekends were simply extended study sessions. As time approached for her to enter a doctoral program, she identified gaps in her academic preparation. Her remedy: summer classes in calculus and economics.

What got her through that stressful three year period? "I was so busy taking classes that I didn't think about it," she jokes. In fact, her mother's vantage point provided her with all the motivation Dr. Andrews needed. "She had worked with professors and had seen how they lived and worked. She always told me, 'Those professors have it so good; if you get that Ph.D., many doors will open for you.'"

And what did she sacrifice during that tough time? "Nothing important. Just hanging out with friends."

The rigorous routine established the standard for her doctoral program at Michigan State, where Dr. Andrews was well prepared for long hours and new challenges. One came along when she learned, late in the game, that she needed to change her dissertation topic—it had already been covered by someone else. She tacked another year onto her timetable.

Previously, she was a professor at the same school where she earned her MBA, Wayne State. She is now a Clinical Assistant Professor of Accounting at Indiana University-Purdue University and, she reports, "It is everything I had hoped it would be—and more."

The dream continues...

A new door opened for Dr. Andrews in 2010, when she took a sabbatical from Wayne State University and served as an Academic Fellow with the Securities and Exchange Commission. She was able to put her computer programming skills learned in her Ph.D. program to good use in the Division of Corporation Finance. As an Assistant Professor, she has actively mentored several undergraduates and guided them toward internships that led to employment. "I try to stress the importance of an internship to them even if it means extending their graduation date," she says. "I tell them they would rather have a full time position at graduation rather than be seeking a full time position."

To MBA or not to MBA, II?

Dr. Brett Gilbert
Rutgers University
Ph.D. Indiana University, management

Once Dr. Brett Gilbert decided to pursue an advanced degree in business, she cut right to the chase. She bypassed earning an MBA, focusing sharply on her ultimate goal. She enrolled directly in a Ph.D. program.

And, like many others who had reached similar decisions before her, she soared. "Having an MBA does not necessarily help you in a doctoral program. You do need a good understanding of business, and an MBA makes sense if you don't have that foundation," she explains. "But I had already gained that understanding from my undergraduate degree and work experiences. At no point in my doctoral program did I feel that my peers with MBAs had any advantage over me."

The decision to skip an MBA came easily to Dr. Gilbert as she analyzed her reasons for seeking an advanced degree— she wanted to do research. Originally, she had planned to earn the master's degree so she could refocus her career on market research. It was while contemplating a return to school that she received a postcard from The PhD Project. Attending the program's annual conference, she learned for the first time that research was central to a professor's life.

78

"When you do research for a company, you have to do it on topics that it is interested in. When I learned that as a professor I could research topics that were of interest to me, combine that with teaching, and get paid for doing it—I thought, 'Wow, this is it!'"

Examining her interests, she concluded that, "This was what God was calling me to do." She re-took the GMAT and applied mostly to schools in areas where costs of living were manageable. Although Indiana University preferred applicants to have an MBA degree, it wisely took a chance with Dr. Gilbert's application.

She went on to become the first entrepreneurship Ph.D. graduate from the school, and her dissertation on the implications of geographic clusters—places such as the Raleigh-Durham area, Silicon Valley, and Hollywood—on new firm performance, was a finalist for an Academy of Management award.

As an associate instructor at Indiana, Dr. Gilbert received top-level teaching evaluations. She continues to do well in her teaching and research efforts. "I can honestly say I love my life," she says. "As a professor you have so much flexibility and autonomy. You can really do the things you want to do. I wouldn't trade it for anything else."

The dream continues…

Now an Associate Professor at Rutgers University, Dr. Gilbert continues to do research that is of great personal interest. Her interests led to an appointment by Texas Governor Rick Perry to serve on the Texas Emerging Technology Fund Advisory Committee while she was on Faculty at Texas A&M University. And in 2009, she received a $50,000 Kauffman Junior Faculty Fellowship, which so far has only been given to 10 emerging scholars in entrepreneurship. She has six published articles to her credit. She has taught in a special program at Texas A&M that helps disabled veterans learn how to start their own businesses. "It is truly a great feeling to have a direct and immediate influence in helping someone's dream come true," Dr. Gilbert says.

For the soul – at any age

Dr. T. Maurice Lockridge
Ph.D. University of Memphis, accounting

At a time in life when many of his peers and friends were planning retirement, Maurice Lockridge was grinding out his doctoral dissertation. "I had to be the oldest Ph.D. student they ever had," says now-professor Lockridge. Although he entered the University of Memphis doctoral program in his forties and was in his fifties when he completed, the idea had been germinating for many years. It may have started in his undergraduate days, when he told a professor he planned to become an accountant. "That's OK," she replied, "but what are you going to do for your soul?"

The words echoed in his mind when, a few years later, a supermarket checkout clerk asked him one day, "You're a preacher, aren't you?"

Dr. Lockridge had to confess that although he was the son of a preacher, his current profession was accountant. "Well," she told him, "You missed your calling. You were meant to spread the word."

Not long after that, Dr. Lockridge set out on the road that would eventually lead to a professorship—without even realizing it at first. After serving as a corporate controller for several companies, he accepted a position as the senior financial officer of the Oakland, California public schools. In this new role, which he started at age forty, he soon came to realize—by observing indirectly—that "teaching was the greatest job on the planet."

His undergraduate professor's words came back to mind, and he resolved to pursue a second career in front of the classroom. The college classroom was where he intended to make his mark. "I want to do something for my soul," he says today. "I've had a very good life."

Although he sacrificed financially and invested many years in earning his doctorate—teaching college without a degree for three years to cover his bills—Dr. Lockridge believes the reward for his patience and persistence has been incalculable.

"I enjoy that moment when you see that the students are 'getting it,'" he says. "What's the good of having knowledge if you don't pass it along? I have something, and it would be a shame for it to die along with me."

The dream continues...
Dr. Lockridge joined the faculty at Marshall University in 2006. He was part of the faculty senate as an assistant chair for the department of Accountancy and Legal environment, before retiring.

The mathematics of life

Dr. Helen Brown- Liburd
Rutgers University
Ph.D University of Wisconsin, Madison, accounting

The reminders would arrive in Helen Brown's mailbox, like clockwork, every year. The wrong time of year, as far as she was concerned.

"Those PhD Project mailings would always come at bonus time," recalls the erstwhile corporate and Big Four accountant.

The message in those PhD Project brochures was seeping into her consciousness, but next to the bonus check, it played second fiddle. For a while. And then Helen Brown embarked on a path that would ultimately answer a question from the textbook on the mathematics of life.

With seventeen years of corporate service already rung up, no dependents, and an unsatisfied but undefined yearning to find deeper meaning in work, how long does it take to turn a career and a life around?

For Dr. Helen Brown, the answer was two years.

"I enjoyed supervising and training people at work, so I had always thought, as many people in business do, 'Maybe I'll teach some classes in the evening at the local university, then when I retire I'll do more.' I was thinking of it in a very limited way."

Two years of lining up The PhD Project's challenge against her six-figure salary and bonus led to Dr. Brown's life-changing epiphany. "That's how long it took," she says, "for me to stop thinking about what I would be losing and start thinking about what I would be gaining."

"I realized that it was the money that was keeping me in the corporation. When I asked myself what I was looking for in life, I had to be honest and say it wasn't corporate America. Then I asked myself, 'Why are you reducing it to money—can't you live on a stipend for five years?' I was single, my only responsibility was to Helen. Once I stopped thinking of it as a financial decision, it became a no-brainer."

Another lesson in the mathematics of life. Dr. Brown had been living beneath her means for several years, and was debt-free. With money removed from her personal equation, what was holding her back? Her comfort zone.

"I had lived in New York all my life; my family was there. It would be facing the unknown…. It was, 'Can you really do this?' It was fear of failure. In seventeen years I was always at least somewhat in control of my environment. Going back to school meant giving up that control."

And she knew, should she hit a rough spot, her support system in New York would be far away.

That was when mathematics surfaced again, as Dr. Brown added it all up and concluded, "It wasn't a big enough reason to avoid earning my Ph.D. I wanted it more than I feared it."

Earning a paycheck as her reward for long, hard hours of work was one thing. Earning inner satisfaction for herself as a professor was something bigger and better. Dr. Brown left her job and was accepted at the University of Wisconsin, Madison. When she graduated, twenty-five friends and family members came from New York City to cheer her on.

Dr. Brown was previously a professor at Boston College. There, she had counseled and advised numerous students, of all races and backgrounds, on career decisions and plans. Should they go for an MBA or go to work? What about this company, or that one? Students who take her freshman level course resurface two or three years later, preparing to enter the job market, to seek her guidance and insights on employers and on career issues.

"Now," says Dr. Brown in a satisfied voice, "I have my dream job."

The dream continues...

Dr. Brown- Liburd's career continues to be her "dream job" as she teaches auditing and accounting information systems at Rutgers University and conducts research on auditor-client negotiations and other topics. Previously, at Boston College, she served as faculty adviser to the campus unit of AHANA, an organization that helps minorities attain success in business careers. "I enjoy my job; it is the right job for me," she says. "When disappointments come along, as they do in any profession, they are part of the process. You pick yourself up and start again."

Fulfilling

Dr. Constance Porter
Rice University
Ph.D. Georgia State University, marketing

The dollars—offers of them, that is—were flying at Constance Porter.

Comfortably situated in a prominent management consulting firm, she found herself the object of an unsolicited, escalating bidding war by two companies seeking to recruit her. The offers were growing increasingly attractive. Uncertain of how to respond, she sought her father for guidance. What she heard was the same message he had delivered to her many times before: "Do what you find fulfilling, not what pays the most. Follow your heart instead of the money."

Two weeks after sharing his advice, Constance Porter's father, Albert, died unexpectedly, leaving a void in her life—but a direction as well. She followed his suggestion and accepted the offer that felt like the best fit.

Two years passed, and another family member altered the course of Dr. Porter's life. Her sister Monica received a mailing about The PhD Project—not the right career move for her, but she knew right away to pick up the phone and tell Constance. "I told her, 'No way; it makes no sense financially,'" Dr. Porter says.

It wasn't the first time Dr. Porter had rebuffed the idea of becoming a business professor. Eight years earlier while earning her MBA, a doctoral student observing her passion for researching, learning, and sharing knowledge, had offered exactly the same suggestion. On that occasion, she declined the advice on grounds that she believed in academia she would grow "out of touch with the real world."

But now, after initially dismissing her sister's call, Dr. Porter heard her father's words replaying in her mind. Examining her career, she had to admit that corporate life might not be her true calling. "I asked myself, wasn't there something a little more challenging and intellectually stimulating?" For Dr. Porter, the answer was "Yes!"

"I had done some soul-searching about the types of activities that ignited my passion. Learning was at the top of the list. Sharing knowledge was also there."

Suddenly she had no doubts as to what step to take. "Sometimes," she says, "you know it just feels right." She attended The PhD Project conference. There, she met faculty members who were passionate about learning as scholars, and teaching as mentors. "Their excitement and passion, along with their willingness to explain the details of the Ph.D. process, hooked me. I knew, from the moment I left, that I was going to do it.

"I had never taught, but in consulting I was always teaching. And I was excited about research possibilities," she explains. "It just made too much sense, and it wasn't about the money. What got me to my decision was realizing I was not born a wealthy person. I wasn't afraid of getting a smaller paycheck, and I knew there was something more important than a salary."

Far from living in poverty, Dr. Porter is a professor at the University of Notre Dame, where her concerns about withdrawal from the business world have proved unfounded. She integrates "real world" examples into the classroom and her research consistently. The appreciative e-mails she receives from students, sometimes years after they have taken her class, attest to the impact she is already exerting. Female minority students tell her they are motivated simply by her presence. "I push my students to think as hard as they can, even if they hate it at the moment," she says.

"People are surprised when I tell them I did not always have the dream of getting a Ph.D. I truly am the quintessential academic," Dr. Porter says. "I love to be thinking about the 'why's of the world."

"All I want to do in life is fulfill my greater purpose— God's plan for me in the world. I understand that, via this profession, I am a positive influence on the lives of many others. Indeed, in my best moments in this profession, I act as a servant to others. I feel good about that."

The dream continues…

Dr. Porter continues to influence students and bring real-world cases into her classroom, now at Rice University. She has conducted and published research on relationship marketing, virtual communities, and other topics. Since 2005, she has been a member of the Editorial Review Board of the Journal of Consumer Affairs, and she currently serves on the Board of Directors of KidsPeace, a nonprofit organization serving kids in crisis.

"Out-of-body" experience yields deal of lifetime

Dr. Byron Hollowell
Black Hills State University
Ph.D. Florida State University, finance

Wall Street investment banker Byron Hollowell, working ninety hours a week during the go-go 90's on some of the planet's hottest deals, sometimes paused to wonder about the long-term benefits of the mergers and acquisitions he was helping to arrange.

When he did, his manager would tell him, "Hollowell, you need to get busy, and don't think about that."

But he did think about it. And while investment banking's furious pace "hardly allowed time for soul-searching and introspection," Byron Hollowell's mind flashed back to the professor who had encouraged him as an undergraduate to consider college teaching one day.

"Back then, he saw me as professor material but I thought basically it was a joke—the farthest thing from my mind. I knew I was headed for Wall Street."

Today, Professor Byron Hollowell recognizes that "it is critical to have someone identify you as having the potential for academe," and he performs that role for many of the students he teaches. He has already guided several to explore the feasibility of becoming a business professor.

When Wall Street hotshot Hollowell reflected back on his mentor's suggestion, he realized why the professor had steered him to classes in math and communications. "He was setting me up to get a Ph.D."

Around the time his questioning about Wall Street's deals grew stronger, Dr. Hollowell learned of The PhD Project. He had often before tutored younger students, and had derived immense satisfaction from it. At the eleventh hour for the program's annual conference deadline, he filled out his application.

The computer crashed, wiping out all traces of his application. There was no time to redo it. "I had to think about that for one year, and because I'd missed out, it stayed in my mind."

During that year, he reestablished contact with his former college mentor, who connected him with other professors so that he could learn more about the academic life. When the following year arrived, Dr. Hollowell applied early to the PhD Project conference.

The conference excited him and impressed him, but he told everyone he met there, "This is great, but I'm not giving up my job."

But upon returning home to New York, Dr. Hollowell underwent what he now describes with a smile as "my out-of-body" experience.

"I found myself somehow filling out these applications and asking people for references. Someone was doing it outside of me. And then it became something I had to do. I was stunned when I realized I had completed the application process."

Back on Wall Street, "All my friends said to me, 'You're going to do *what?* For *how* long?'"

Dr. Hollowell knew that he'd be making a short-term financial tradeoff by leaving boomtown. But he also knew it was the smartest deal he had ever done. It was the one for himself.

Moving into graduate housing to cut costs and focus himself fully on studies, Dr. Hollowell breezed through his doctoral program in four years. Weighing the long hours he worked on Wall Street, he now realizes "I'm really not losing that much as a professor."

Meanwhile, he has already started giving back. "When I was a college student," he recalls, "I had so much given to me. I went in with the sole ambition of getting a job where I would not be laid off. And forty-three professors worked on me, sending me to internships and co-ops, to study abroad. I was fundamentally a different person when I came out. Now, I want to pay back some of the debt that was created when my professors went out of their way to empower me."

Like the football player who got a C on one paper, along with a "please come see me" note from Dr. Hollowell. He told the young man, "You are not a C student. You are an A student. Let's look at some strategies to get you there."

Stunned, the student told him, "No one has ever done this to me before." The student earned straight A's the rest of the semester.

"You never know the effect of a pebble in a pond, where the ripples will go," says Dr. Hollowell—who, in addition to inspiring students, is conducting research into a wide range of areas.

Including, of course, the long-term consequences of Wall Street mergers and acquisitions.

The dream continues...

Now an Associate Professor at Black Hills State University, Dr. Hollowell leverages his Wall Street experience as director of the university's Student Investment Fund, an educational and investment experience for students. He was a finalist for the Penn State University Campus Teaching Excellence Award and recipient of its highest research honor. He has published eleven articles on the long-term effects of mergers and acquisitions. He regularly shares in class the challenges faced by African Americans and women in the highly technical fields in the corporate world. In addition, he admonishes women and minorities to seek out upwardly mobile positions in accounting and finance. Recently a student wrote to him, "I learned more from you within the ten minutes of interview prep than I did with most professors over the course of fourteen weeks."

Other-mindedness

Dr. Andrea Scott
Pepperdine University
Ph.D. University of Southern Florida, marketing

 The booming 1990s were a heady, exciting time to be an advertising executive for Fortune 500 companies and top agencies. But for Andrea Scott, there was an unsettling undercurrent to those go-go years. She subscribed to a viewpoint she calls "other-mindedness," and she wasn't seeing enough of it in her environment.

"I was troubled by the atmosphere of 'everyone out for oneself,'" she remembers today. "When you train for business, sometimes it cultivates a narrow-mindedness. My background and heart was in social marketing: sharing the wealth, educating people, and cultivating some sense of awareness of others."

Somewhat interested in returning to academia for a terminal degree some day, she pursued a successful marketing career under the mistaken belief that business professors only taught as a sideline. Then, at the National Black MBA Association conference, she met some professors associated with The PhD Project and learned for the first time about the opportunities of earning a business doctorate. What she heard made her heart jump: not only could she gain a platform to inspire a generation of future business leaders in other-mindedness, but "I loved the fact that I could research whatever interested me."

Dr. Scott knew that with her combination of creative experience, an international background (she was born and raised in Jamaica), and her others-oriented world view, she would have something special to offer students. "My other-mindedness stems from coming from a poor country. It was a place that had a 'we' rather than 'I' mentality, a greater sense of belonging to a community. I have always been conscious of the opportunity and obligation to look beyond myself."

Having made her decision, Dr. Scott marched determinedly through her Ph.D. studies, completed a Fulbright grant to her native Jamaica, and went on to a marketing faculty position at Pepperdine University. There, she uses real-life examples from the news, nonprofit organization case studies, and from her personal experience in community activity to help make marketing more accessible. She engages her students in group projects to give them experiences in encountering—and learning from—other people whose perspectives and viewpoints differ from their own.

"We talk in class about doing charity, about corporate sponsorship issues, and we think about them. We don't skip those chapters."

The dream continues…

Dr. Scott's project exploring the challenges of successful HIV/AIDS communication in her native Jamaica won grants and was published and presented. She keynoted an academic seminar in Jamaica in 2006. She also reports, "My commitment to other-mindedness continues. International students in particular seek me out as they know that their perspective and outlook will be appreciated, even sought out, in our classroom conversations." She adds, "I find it interesting that more and more students who come to me for career (and life) counseling are longing to find purpose in their chosen profession. I am encouraged that they see my own passion for what I do and often ask what led me to teaching and researching."

92

When five becomes eight

Dr. Nichole Castater
Barry University
Ph.D. University of South Carolina, finance

The Berlin Wall was falling, and Nichole Castater was right there. An undergraduate studying German abroad for a semester, she had chosen Berlin, and found herself witnessing history unfolding. The excitement in the air was palpable that year, and it caught Dr. Castater, carrying her in a new career direction—one in which she would help privatized companies in the former Soviet bloc create business plans.

After several such engagements, she observed that Eastern European entrepreneurs seemed to reserve their deepest respect for any Western consultant whose name ended in "Ph.D." Having long wanted to become a college professor one day, Dr. Castater fine-tuned her career plan—she would earn her doctorate in business, and add teaching and researching on newly-privatized businesses to her consulting work with them.

The plan unfolded as she had hoped—until, working on her dissertation, the cold, hard rigors of academic research methodology collided with the realities of freewheeling Eastern European businesses. Detailed data on the businesses she was analyzing simply did not exist—standard Western accounting practices not having fully taken hold in the former Iron Curtain economies—and her research was stymied.

Dr. Castater had to recast and restructure her dissertation plan. She devised another route, but the meter was running—eventually adding three years to her doctoral program. Three years of deferring the day when she would be entitled to earn the title and financial compensation of a professor. Three more years of living on a student budget.

"It was an incredible financial sacrifice," she says, "but it will be well worth it in the end. I will have a great deal of autonomy, I will be doing what I love, and I hope to teach for as long as I can."

Dr. Castater deployed a number of strategies to get her through the additional three years of investment. She went after them at full bore—having determined she needed to secure additional funding sources, she sought and won a Fulbright.

She also found other grants and never said no to any teaching or research opportunity that came her way. Student loans helped bridge the gap. Finally, while completing the dissertation, she set emotions aside and obtained a teaching position at another university because it offered higher compensation.

Dr. Castater's advice for negotiating the years of financial investment as a doctoral student: "Look for grants within your university. Realize that student loans are not the big bad things people think they are—interest rates are low. Do not charge everything on your credit card—it becomes formidable."

And, finally: "Make sure your dissertation and doctoral program take first priority. Make sure you get it done. When you do, more opportunities are open to you by far."

Today, Dr. Castater, having followed her own advice, says, "I am now getting to the point where I want to be—doing what I want to do, on my own terms, at a place I love."

The dream continues...
Now an Associate Professor of Finance at Barry University (Miami Shores, FL), Dr. Castater is also Associate Editor of the Journal of International Business Review and Practices. With her late husband, Dr. Robert Ware III, she authored and published an article on "Virtuality and Stock Price" in that publication. She has served as Secretary and Program Chair for the Academy of International Business—Midwest. She has researched and presented on the topic of transparency and corporate governance in the private military industry.

When a big salary isn't enough

Dr. Melvin Smith
Case Western Reserve University
Ph.D. University of Pittsburgh, management

As he contemplated shifting gears in his life plan radically—from high-powered, hefty-salaried corporate executive to the professorial podium of academia—Melvin Smith made a big mistake.

He assumed that becoming a management professor would slash his income drastically and permanently.

But, several years later, Dr. Smith not only leads a comfortable life, he earns nearly as much as he did in his days of strolling the executive corridors of IBM, Pepsico, and Heinz. And, he reports, his life today is far richer and more fulfilling in countless, often intangible ways.

"There is no big sacrifice financially, especially when you factor in the consulting work a professor can do," he says.

What challenged Dr. Smith financially were those first five years after the big decision—his turn as a doctoral student. But a plan, and a pact with his wife, helped ease the economic and marital stress that many prospective Ph.D. candidates anticipate.

Step one for Dr. Smith, father of two young boys, was promising his wife that the family would not have to uproot and relocate. He enrolled in a doctoral program at the University of

Pittsburgh, close to home. Next, he pledged that the household would not suffer financially during his student days. Like many in the business world, he had assembled a nest egg over the years—intending to dip into it one day and start his own business.

One day became now. "I made the commitment to my wife that we would not sacrifice while I did this. We made no major compromises," Dr. Smith says. The nest egg helped stabilize the family budget during his student days, with his wife continuing to work.

Dr. Smith also took the unusual step in his doctoral program's latter stages of adding some part time consulting work with a former employer—while remaining a full time student. "I knew I could maintain the same quality of work in school," he reports. "I would just give up some sleep."

All it took was some careful scheduling—and a strong dose of determination. From 8:00 a.m. until 6:00 p.m. most days, Melvin Smith cracked the books as a student and researcher. From 6:00 until 10:00 p.m. nightly was family time. And then, as the family slept, he would hunch over his computer and handle consulting assignments until the early morning hours.

The end result today is a new career that offers Dr. Smith all the autonomy, intellectual challenge, and work-life balance that he had hoped to achieve. And, for Mrs. Smith, the outcome is a happier, more fulfilled husband—one who has found time to help send the boys off to school each morning, coach Little League, and attend all those soccer, basketball, and football games that would have been missed in his corporate life.

Nor, he adds, did attaining a balance require a drop down to professional mediocrity in exchange. Dr. Smith has co-authored a book chapter with two prominent scholars in his field, and the National Black MBA Association honored him as a top doctoral student.

Looking back on the fateful decision to switch careers, Dr. Smith says, "I was in a position that some might have seen as being locked—into that corporate track. But I showed it was possible."

The dream continues...
His young boys are now young men, with the oldest in his third year at the University of Michigan and the youngest in his final year of high school. Dr. Smith has enjoyed being able to faithfully attend their sporting events, band performances, and numerous other activities over the years. "I have ended up working just as many hours as I did in the corporate world, but I have had much more flexibility over when and where I work many of those hours. And, the work has been much more meaningful." Dr. Smith is now a Professor of Organizational Behavior and Faculty Director of Executive Education at Case Western Reserve University, Weatherhead School of Management. His teaching is focused largely on executives, both here in the U.S. and abroad. He also continues to conduct research and mentor doctoral students, as well as being an active public speaker.

98

The investment

Dr. Kendra Harris
Ph.D. George Washington University, marketing

Through more than five intense years as a doctoral student, Kendra Harris could not help but notice that her old friends in corporate life were driving newer cars, and living in bigger houses, than she was. And every time a former colleague jetted off for another lavish vacation, she needed to check in with her inner value system for reaffirmation.

There, she found all the reward she needed: "My self worth," she explains, "is not tied to my financial status."

But now that she is Dr. Kendra Harris, a new awareness has crept in: not only is she more fulfilled in her new career, but she earns more now than she would have by remaining at the Fortune 500 company she chose to leave.

The irony is sweet. Having left corporate America to find more meaning in life, her short-term financial sacrifice for doctoral studies has revealed itself a wise long-term investment.

Kendra Harris might have missed the turn in her life's road that led to her current deeply satisfying position. Twice before, she deliberately rejected the notion of earning a Ph.D.

In fact, she first dismissed the idea at an age when most children have never even heard of a doctoral degree.

"Back when I was a child in elementary school, I had a relative who wrote a dissertation. I looked at this one hundred-page document and said, 'I'll never get a Ph.D. I couldn't write a hundred page paper.'"

A few years later as an undergraduate, she grew accustomed to writing lengthy papers, and she acquired the itch to teach business in college. But once again, she vowed not to pursue a doctorate. "I thought, 'I'll get my MBA,' and I did. I thought again, 'I'll never go back to school.'"

Kendra Harris entered corporate life, "but that calling to teach kept tugging and tugging at me."

She taught without a doctoral degree at two colleges before the eventful moment when her dean connected her with the dean and doctoral program head of George Washington University business school. Sizing up her strengths, they came to the inevitable conclusion—they invited her to apply to their doctoral program.

The light came on: Kendra Harris finally realized the time had arrived for her to become Dr. Harris.

First, she had to get over the short-term hurdle of committing herself to several years of greatly reduced income. She found the decision surprisingly easy. "I always had the philosophy that as long as I was involved in my passion, the money would come. I knew that at a point, I would reap the fruits of my labor."

The fancy cars and toys her corporate friends were amassing—"the perks of being a successful professional"—did not sway her.

"All of that," she says, "would have to go into a holding pattern. What's meant to be mine is going to be mine, and what's meant to be yours is going to be yours. When it's my turn, it will be my turn."

Now that her turn has come, Dr. Harris reflects back and observes that "a very high quality network of family and friends who always gave me faith and wisdom" was more valuable than a set of keys to a new car.

As a teacher, Dr. Harris has influenced students to major in marketing, and to pursue MBAs. One undergrad told her, "I wouldn't have made it through without you."

"That," says Dr. Harris, "definitely makes you feel that you are in the right place."

The dream continues...

Kendra Harris served as Lead Professor of Business Administration and Lead Professor of Marketing. She was voted Students' Choice Teacher of the Year in the School of Business in 2008, and won a university-wide teaching excellence award that carried a monetary stipend and the privilege of competing for a North Carolina Governor's Teaching Award. She won a Chancellor's Concept Paper Contest. She is not currently in academia.

His own path

Dr. Ronald Ramirez
University of Colorado, Denver
Ph.D. University of California Irvine,
management information systems

In eight years as an operations and finance manager in Fortune 500 companies, Ronald Ramirez saw his employers invest vast sums of money in new information technologies. Despite the benefits generated from using the technology, it was often unclear how to measure the actual return on these large investments. Ramirez grew eager to look deeper into this but in corporate life, he knew, time is scarce, and "there is always another fire to put out."

Still, he could not shake his interest in this compelling question, and he was determined to look further into it. Happily, he now does so as Professor Ronald Ramirez.

"I am now more fulfilled than I have ever been in my career," he reports. "Now I can focus on topics that truly interest me. That does not often happen in a corporation, given time constraints and the business at hand. Corporate America also limits your own individual efforts to research such questions as work days now often extend into your personal time.

"Here in the university, you have the opportunity to control your own research topics, your classroom, and your hours. You set the terms."

While an academic career offers many benefits, deciding to begin the journey as a Ph.D. student was nonetheless difficult. "I was just starting to hit my stride in the business world," he recounts. "I was five years out of my MBA program, and I was being considered for a promotion to Finance Director at my company. However, I had reached a point where I was unfulfilled. After attending the first PhD Project conference in 1994, I had labored over the decision to pursue a Ph.D. for several years. I just could not put it off any longer. I knew there had to be something else."

A major obstacle: accepting that his income would take a hit during his doctoral studies. In addition, salaries in high technology companies can be significantly higher than those in academe. Dr. Ramirez does not mind. "The ability to do research motivates people in this field more than the financial rewards. I am more interested in research and its personal rewards, so I put it above everything else. You have to come to terms with the income issue before you enter a Ph.D. program and an academic career. If you can look beyond the financial aspects, you can find an unmatched level of career happiness as a professor."

An unexpected bonus of his new academic life is the discovery that classroom instruction is "very rewarding."

"I have many years of real world experience," he explains, "and it gives me an advantage in the classroom. I can apply real world examples to the concepts and theories introduced in textbooks. More importantly, students are at an age where they need both academic and career guidance. I have plenty of advice for my students as I have had my share of success and disappointment over the years. It feels good to be able to give something back."

The dream continues...

Dr. Ramirez, continuing to create and follow his own path, has been published extensively and presented at numerous conferences, on such topics as IT diffusion, innovation, and the impact of IT investment on innovation and productivity. In 2005, he received a research development grant from the University of California, Irvine.

"The landlord"

Dr. Ricardo Valerdi
University of Arizona
Ph.D. University of Southern California,
information systems

Ricardo Valerdi was the only doctoral student in his program—and probably the state—who spent evenings repairing broken plumbing pipes and fixing faulty electrical wiring.

The unusual nocturnal activities were the result of a creative, if occasionally nerve-racking strategy he devised to pay the bills during his doctoral studies.

Having chosen to trade a lucrative paycheck and career in engineering at a Fortune 100 company for the austere life of a doctoral student—"A large bureaucratic corporation is not a place for lots of creativity, and I still hungered for that" —he listened thoughtfully as his boss told him, "You're crazy for quitting your job."

Dr. Valerdi knew what his boss was thinking. "To do what I did, you have to change your financial lifestyle. You can't afford the house or the vacation. And a car is out of the question."

But the soon-to-be ex-engineer had a plan. Rather than sell his San Diego townhouse, he refinanced it and used the proceeds to buy a duplex in Los Angeles, four blocks from USC. He lived downstairs and rented out the upper apartment. With the rental income from that and the San Diego home, he was living nearly rent-free—if occasionally bound to handyman duties.

"I was the only landlord in my Ph.D. program," Dr. Valerdi says with a note of pride. "And I did this as a student in probably the most expensive real estate market in the country." The plan was orchestrated carefully—it would have all fallen apart had he failed to lock in his mortgage commitment while still employed and bringing home a respectable paycheck.

Meanwhile, the new financial constraints were more than offset by a new career that seemed limitless. "With a Ph.D. in IS the sky's the limit," he says. "You can teach, do research, and consult. In my corporate job, I was one of forty thousand engineers. Now I am one of four thousand Ph.D.s in the nation. Your sphere of influence as a professor is at a completely different level of impact."

Dr. Valerdi credits his father, a Ph.D. in engineering, with modeling an academic career and influencing his choice. Off to a fast start, Dr. Valerdi completed his program in three years, publishing two journal articles in the process. And, as a fringe benefit, his timing was perfect: the duplex that financed his doctoral program doubled in value during the time he lived there. Now that he again earns a "real" paycheck, he has grown his small real estate empire to four properties.

The dream continues...

Dr. Valerdi, no longer distracted by the need to moonlight as a handyman, has published eleven journal articles and presented thirty-six conference papers. One paper won a "best paper" award at a 2005 conference. He is co-editor of a new journal, Journal of Enterprise Transformation. Dr. Valerdi created a new class at Massachusetts Institute of Technology, where he taught formerly, on cost estimation and measurement systems, and mentors undergraduate and graduate students. He serves on the editorial advisory board of the Journal of Enterprise Information Systems. He is also working toward a Masters degree in psychology at Harvard University.

More than the money

Dr. Ulysses Brown
Savannah State University
Ph.D. Jackson State University, management

Seeking out a new career path upon retiring from the Navy, Ulysses Brown taught middle school for a while, then enrolled in advanced graduate studies in psychology. Along the way, he began assisting a faculty member in research. One day the professor pulled him aside and asked, "Do you know the difference between a Ph.D. in psychology and one in business?"

"I was looking for something profound," Dr. Brown remembers. But the professor's answer was short and simple.

"He told me, 'the difference is about $35,000 a year.'" The professor now had his student's full attention. "I did some checking, and I came back to him the next day," Dr. Brown recalls, "and said, 'alright, what do I have to do?'"

As things turned out, the differences turned out to be more than financial. Within days of arriving as a business doctoral candidate at Jackson State, a historically Black college, Dr. Brown was teaching. Instantly, he became a role model to thirty-five undergraduates. Influencing them in the classroom would not be enough. So he added an unofficial topic to the syllabus: career opportunities in academia and the federal government.

Originally on the faculty at Florida A&M, Dr. Brown lifted his mentoring profile to new heights. He opened an informal mentoring program outside class hours to train any willing student in research methodology. "I bought a computer for them in my office, and I showed them how to enter data and analyze it. I showed them how to write."

Several of the students who crowded around Dr. Brown's computer have since had their work published. Another group of students completed their research papers and had them accepted for presentation at academic conferences. Five students have gone on to graduate studies as a direct result of the after-class sessions in Dr. Brown's office, and others are preparing to do the same.

There was no choice in being a role model. Dr. Brown says, "Whether you want to be or not, you are. I realized how influential it had been for me to do research with that faculty member I worked with, and I thought, 'why don't I do it here?'"

Dr. Brown also encourages his students to consider emulating his track and becoming a professor. "If you are going to make $75,000 a year in a corporation, why not do it in academia, not have to work twelve months a year, and get to attend PTA meetings and school plays?"

Flexibility in setting his own agenda has turned out to be one of the key benefits of a professor's life for Dr. Brown. He teaches four classes, with a schedule that frees him to pursue research from his home office two days a week. "I don't know that there is any other place where I could make the kind of money I earn, and do what I like," he says with satisfaction.

The dream continues...

Dr. Brown is now a Full Professor of Management at Savannah State University. His current research addresses organizational performance of military units, student ethics, and advanced research methods. He has received several awards for research and has published more than fifty refereed journal publications and conference proceedings. He developed a course that teaches research skills to students interested in attending graduate school. With him, they have presented papers at national and international conferences, several of which have been

108

published in refereed journals. Former students of the course have entered graduate programs in business, law, and public administration.

The fear factor

Dr. Jose Castillo
University of Arkansas at Pine Bluff
Ph.D. University of Texas Pan American, management

Dr. Jose Castillo calls it the Fear Factor: the intimidation and resistance that sometimes kicks in when a newly-minted MBA, eager to explore earning a doctorate and advancing to a professorship, contemplates the realities of not returning to the corporate world.

"You are secure in the notion that you can earn a living after having gotten your MBA. And then you compare it to the notion that you are about to immerse yourself into that which has just made you poor." But Dr. Castillo, after earning his MBA, realized that immersing himself in the realm of ideas "became more important than going back to the job market." He found programs and scholarships to defray the costs of pursuing a doctorate, but he was initially turned down—as an applicant to attend The PhD Project conference, and by the doctoral program that ultimately accepted him. The rejections, he says, "helped me. I said, 'I'm going to have to prove these people wrong.'"

Having done so, Dr. Castillo today says, "I continue to be charged by what got me there—the pursuit of ideas and research."

110

The dream continues...

Dr. Castillo is now Associate Professor of Business Administration at University of Arkansas at Pine Bluff. He received a Distinguished Researcher Award and has been published extensively, and he takes great pride in having guided two Hispanic students into doctoral programs. "I think being told 'no' or that one does not 'measure up' or 'doesn't belong' are very good extrinsic motivators that just add fuel to the fire that burns brightly within oneself. I've been told 'no' many times and I just love proving people wrong," he says.

Finding a balance

"Dr. Mommy"

Dr. Darlene Motley
Chatham University
Ph.D. University of Pittsburgh, management

Enjoying a successful career at some of America's best-known companies, Darlene Motley paused to reflect upon getting married.

"I knew I wanted children, and I was traveling a lot. I did not want both of us to be working long hours and traveling all the time.

"I wrestled over how to make the job fit, and then I realized that I could make a difference, have children, and have flexibility—if I became a business professor."

Dr. Darlene Motley has already achieved all three goals.

"I was pregnant with my first child during my comprehensive exams. I didn't want anyone to know because I didn't want them to think I was looking for sympathy. My children are now ten and nine, and they call me "Dr. Mommy."

As "Dr. Mommy," she repeatedly fine-tunes the balancing act and makes accommodations in her professional life "so I can be there for my children's programs when I want to, not when I can."

To better control her time, she chose employment at a university where teaching is the primary focus. Research is a part of the process, but not with the same emphasis.

She has rejected, sometimes reluctantly, opportunities to do work overseas—opportunities she now looks forward to pursuing, with her children getting older. And when her department asked her to serve on two committees, she said "yes" to one and "no" to another.

"I greatly appreciate the ability to say 'no,' and not have it be a detriment," she says.

It has taken Dr. Motley ten years to reach the salary level she had attained before leaving corporate life. "I had to ask myself, what else is it that draws me to this," she says.

"I knew I could be making more money in business, but I would not be as happy, and I would not have the flexibility that comes with academia."

The dream continues...

Following her success over the years, Dr. Motley now serves as the Dean of the School of Arts, Science & Business at Chatham University. In 2005, Dr. Motley became director of the M.S. in Human Resource Management program at Robert Morris University. She was instrumental in developing and launching the program. She received tenure, became Associate Professor, and in 2008 was appointed department head of management with responsibility for the Undergraduate Business program, the Masters of Science in Human Resource program, and the Masters of Science in Non-profit Management. She also served as the chair of the Ethics Committee for the School of Business and the Diversity Committee of Robert Morris University.

Date nights

Dr. Ariana Pinello
Florida Gulf Coast University
Ph.D. Florida State University, accounting

The e-mail message was one of the longest and most detailed Dr. Ariana Pinello had ever received from a student. It recited countless facts and information bits from a class Dr. Pinello had taught, including some she had herself forgotten—and with good reason: the class had taken place a full year ago.

The student had been an engineering major, until encountering Dr. Pinello. Her enthusiasm for the subject matter, and her belief in his talent, had inspired the young man to switch majors to accounting. He was writing to thank her.

Dr. Pinello has received similar e-mails from other students she has influenced, encouraged, and inspired. The messages she receives are one measure of the impact she has already had in her new career as a professor.

It was a career that came close to never happening. A successful accountant for several years, she had long yearned to return to the intellectual stimulation of academic life. Receiving The PhD Project brochure each year, she thought that the combination of learning and teaching might be her dream job. "The notion of teaching students, of helping them become whatever they want to become, and to actually have a positive influence on someone's life, seemed more gratifying to me than auditing financial statements," she says.

But for someone soon to be married, even the grueling demands of a Big Four accounting firm seemed to pale in comparison to the strain on family life that she had heard a business doctoral program could cause. "I was hearing that a lot of Ph.D. students got divorced during their program, that a marriage could suffer," she recalls. "I thought, is this right for me?"

Part of the potential strain, Dr. Pinello heard from some successful doctoral students, was that Ph.D. candidates can immerse themselves in an intellectual life to the point where the spouse feels left out. Dr. Pinello and her husband-to-be, a physician assistant, had no intention of becoming a divorce statistic. So they fashioned a game plan.

"You have to know when to spend time together," she says. "When one person feels distant, they have to come out and say it. And the other partner has to stop whatever they're doing, and make time to spend together."

Dr. Pinello and her new husband scheduled regular "date nights." She might work all day Saturday, but come Saturday night, they would head out the door together. Breakfasts were chances to share a few minutes over bowls of cereal; sometimes they would even meet for lunch. They honeymooned between semesters in the Caribbean.

When she reached the dissertation stage, her husband helped her collect data. This created an opportunity for them to travel together: "It became an activity we shared." Dr. Pinello believes this conscious effort to make things work at home as much as on campus expanded her ability to succeed.

Now that she is a professor, Dr. Pinello believes she has attained a lifestyle more rewarding than she had dared hope for. In addition to the appreciative students she has influenced, and the papers she has begun publishing, she has more. "I've got intellectual stimulation, a strong relationship with my spouse, and I'm living in a gorgeous home in a city I like.

"I've got autonomy and flexibility. I can work on the projects I want to. I would never have had this life had I not made this change."

116

The dream continues...
Dr. Pinello is now on faculty at Florida Gulf Coast University. She received the 2005 Outstanding Dissertation Award of the Accounting, Behavior, and Organizations Section of the American Accounting Association, and two of her research studies have been published in premier academic journals. "As a professor, I have a lot of autonomy and flexibility in my schedule, especially compared to what my schedule was like in the corporate world," she says. "I still work just as hard, but the flexibility makes all the difference in achieving work-life balance."

Young motivators

Dr. Velvet Weems-Landingham
Kent State University, Geauga
Ph.D. Case Western Reserve University,
management

For some prospective doctoral students, being the parent of young children is grounds to defer taking the plunge for a few years. But for Dr. Velvet Weems-Landingham, having a toddler and an infant was a powerful motivator—and a welcomed source of stress relief.

"Having children pushed me to get through," Dr. Weems-Landingham says. "I realized, 'I have obligations now. I have to get this done.'"

"Besides," she adds, "they became my break from studies, and they gave me joy. You see your children doing something new, and you have to stop and laugh. I truly needed that."

Dr. Weems-Landingham was fortunate to have a relative, whom she hired part time to be with her children, Sable (twenty months) and Carlton (two months). But even with help, she had to master the special balancing act skills of the doctoral student with family commitments.

"I learned how to work in the middle of the night—it is a peaceful time with no one around," she recalls.

No stranger to hard work, Dr. Weems-Landingham had been earning a comfortable six-figure salary, with full perks and often-posh surroundings, as an IT consultant for prominent companies and law firms. Like many other future business professors, she discovered her calling when her corporate bosses assigned her to manage people and projects. "I also was always interested in organizations. I had an inquisitive nature regarding organizations, people, and what made them tick," she notes. "I also had earned both substantial money and experience during my corporate journey, and I wanted to share those experiences and insights with future corporate leaders."

Dr. Weems-Landingham earned her Masters degree from Carnegie Mellon University and was one of the few African-American doctoral students at Case Western Reserve University's Weatherhead School of Management. She now serves as the only African-American female in the department of Management and Information Systems at Kent State University.

"I believe I offer a very different perspective as a Black professor," she says, "and my presence alone signals progress. I am someone who students can talk to about working in industry—tying together theory and application. For Black students and others valuing diversity, they see an African-American professor, and there's a sigh of relief."

Dr. Weems-Landingham has drawn on her years in business, with her broad background as a consultant in various industries, to help many students determine a career direction.

The dream continues...

Dr. Weems-Landingham has presented and published widely on online teaching and learning, and on project management and performance enhancement in virtual teams. Her children, babies when she started her doctoral program, are on track to both be in school as she completes her tenure process. "We have all grown immensely in our knowledge and understanding of the importance and value of the education experience. I look forward to the future and cherish all that has brought me here," she says. Dr. Weems-Landingham has engaged in no fewer than twenty-five separate service activities or committees. Her service includes faculty mentoring, peer review and evaluation, and more.

One city

Dr. Harriette Bettis-Outland
University of West Florida
Ph.D. Georgia State University, marketing

One city. How hard could it be?, IBM executive Harriette Bettis-Outland wondered.

Riding the wave of a successful, ten-year sales and marketing career in computer software, she had begun considering other options when her baby son was born. At the time, she was traveling five days a week—which didn't leave much time to experience, much less enjoy, motherhood.

Dr. Bettis-Outland had harbored a desire to become a professor since her MBA studies. Observing those teachers she admired most, she concluded it would be best to first work in corporate America for several years. That way, she reasoned, she would garner a collection of useful stories to share with her students.

But now she also wanted to tell other kinds of stories— like "Rock-a-bye Baby" and "Twinkle, Twinkle Little Star."

The timing, the urge to enter academia, and the demands of parenthood had all aligned, and Dr. Bettis-Outland started exploring the ins and outs of becoming a doctoral student. The first thing she heard—and the recurring theme she would hear— was how difficult and stressful it was for anyone, and especially a new mother, to pursue a business Ph.D.

But Dr. Bettis-Outland had a broader perspective from all those years of business travel. After routinely crisscrossing the country each week—California today, the East Coast tomorrow—the stress and challenge of a doctoral program couldn't be that intimidating. After all, she would get to do all the work in just one city. Looking at it from that angle, she realized she might not find it so tough after all.

To learn more about the path to a business professorship, Dr. Bettis-Outland attended a PhD Project conference. She left excited and "on fire," she remembers. She also left the conference early to fly home for a party—her son Elliot's first birthday.

In the following weeks, though, she took and retook the GMAT exam, left her job to devote her energy to entering a doctoral program, and began the ritual of applying to schools. "In retrospect, leaving a good job with a one-year-old child was crazy," she recalls, "but sometimes life just works out."

Dr. Bettis-Outland was accepted by one of the schools she coveted most. Her program included an attractive option to take some coop classes at a cross-town university, Georgia State University. To her surprise, she found that State's doctoral program was more attuned to her interests than the one in which she was enrolled. She decided to seek a transfer. Then, around that time, personal tragedy struck: her marriage unraveled. "I was divorcing my husband and my school at the same time," she says. "It was a very stressful time, but I just felt that things were going to work out." Friends and peers she made through The PhD Project called in with words of encouragement constantly. "They were the ones who sustained me," she says. She switched institutions without missing a day of study.

Compounding her challenge, Dr. Bettis-Outland suffered an accident and broke her leg in the semester before comprehensive exams. Getting to school now seemed impossible. She reached out again to a PhD Project colleague— someone also at Georgia State, Constance Porter. Dr. Porter, intently pursuing her own doctorate, squeezed in time to drive her friend to and from class each day, and even to pitch in with picking up Elliot, then seven, on occasion. The leg, the child, and the doctoral student's dreams all came through the challenge intact. That semester, Dr. Bettis-Outland never missed a class—and was never even late.

Dr. Bettis-Outland is now a professor at the University of West Florida. "Getting through took a whole lot of faith and a lot of friends," she says. "Looking back, I was too busy to know what I was doing was crazy. I was used to challenges, and I never paid attention to the negatives."

Having confined the challenges to just one locale, Dr. Bettis-Outland took them on one at a time and conquered them. Not having to step on an airplane made it all seem do-able.

The dream continues...

Dr. Bettis-Outland successfully balances work with life in one location: Pensacola, Florida. 2008 was a standout year for her: she was named Outstanding Faculty Member of the Year by her university's Marketing and Logistics Association, was co-editor of the Journal of Business and Industrial Marketing's special issue on trade show marketing, and received a summer research grant from her university. In 2008, she was elevated from vice chair to co-chair of the American Marketing Association's Relationship Marketing Special Interest Group. She has published three articles and many conference proceedings and presentations since 2003, having overcome the challenge of a hurricane destroying her home in 2004 and forcing her into temporary housing for two years.

Wedding invitation

Dr. Miles Davis
Shenandoah University
Ph.D. George Washington University, management

The contrasts between corporate life and an academic career were drawn starkly in the early 2000s for former business consulting executive Miles Davis, now a professor at Shenandoah University.

Watching his friends and former colleagues endure the stress of a chilly economy, he realized, "I have a multi-year contract, which I never had before. I spent my summer with my kids; my friends spent theirs worrying about having a job.

"I served as the president of the parent teacher organization at my children's school and sat on the board of the local soccer organizations. I have time to balance my life. The quality of life, the stress levels, are very different for me now."

The recipient of a Teacher of the Year award, Dr. Davis becomes engaged in his students' lives.

One woman was consumed with anxiety over what she should do upon graduation. "I took her through the same process I use in organizational strategy for companies, and I applied it to her career: what is your mission statement, what are your objectives, what is your competitive advantage? She got a sense of what she wanted to accomplish for herself."

The student decided to pursue an MBA and was accepted. "Then, she invited me to her wedding. The fact that a student would invite me to her wedding was just incredible to me."

Dr Davis is very conscious of his status as a role model. "We have students here from all over the world. Some have never seen an African-American in any position of authority or responsibility. So, I am conscious that what I do in the class room can impact their perspective of others in organizations." Additionally, Dr. Davis states "that for African-American and other students of colored, my being in front of the class room introduces them to another career option."

"I can't imagine anything better than getting paid for what I love to do—to develop my ideas and share them," says Dr. Davis. "To be an African-American, and celebrated in my community because of my role, is just incredible."

The dream continues…

Dr. Davis was granted tenure and is Associate Professor of Management and the founder and inaugural Director of the Institute for Entrepreneurship at Shenandoah University. He has earned several teaching awards and honors; is Associate Editor of The New England Journal of Entrepreneurship, and host of an award-winning radio show on small business and entrepreneurship; created a program to encourage high school students to become entrepreneurs and is writing a book on entrepreneurs who use faith to guide their business practices. He serves on the boards of his children's school and the local youth soccer league—"activities I would have never been able to undertake if I was still working in the corporate world."

Balancing – and pitching

Dr. Sharron Hunter-Rainey
Langston University
Ph.D. Duke University, management

As a doctoral student in management at Duke University, Sharron Hunter-Rainey absorbed the same pool of knowledge her classmates did. She, however, was the only one also aiming to simultaneously achieve proficiency in camping and baseball.

Juggling home and career for Dr. Hunter-Rainey required some exquisite balancing, because there were three homes. Before enrolling at Duke, she had worked for Frito-Lay in Dallas. Her husband Dennis, an emergency medicine physician, was shuttling back and forth between there and Detroit, where he had both family and work. He needed to remain in his two-city job while Dr. Hunter-Rainey pursued her doctorate. So she and her son, Morgan, then five, moved to Durham, North Carolina, placing her in the role of single mother on weekdays.

"I learned to pitch a tent and pitch a baseball," she remembers with a broad smile.

More critical to her academic work, she also "learned to read anywhere, even on a soccer field."

The balancing act necessitated hard choices and careful planning. Dr. Hunter-Rainey decided to forgo teaching assignments that would have provided extra income. Accepting the work would have cut too deeply into her family life. She also followed a strict regimen. "I woke up each day with a plan. When the sun came up, I knew what I would be doing. I might not get it all done, but what wasn't done became by default the plan for tomorrow."

Succeeding at juggling is more than just good time management, she is quick to point out. "It's knowing your different roles. I'm a wife, a mom, and a teacher. When you're wearing one hat, you play that role to the fullest, and when you switch hats you step into that role totally."

Work-life issues were not the only challenges Dr. Hunter-Rainey had to surmount during her doctoral studies. Before she had gotten through her course work, the two professors she had chosen to work with were both gone. One left in her first year, the other died less than a year later.

But Dr. Hunter-Rainey never wavered or doubted her course. After sixteen years as an engineer and marketer for Procter Gamble and Frito-Lay, and with stellar achievements to her credit—including three patents—she was burning for a new challenge. With many new hires under her supervision, she found herself constantly teaching, and she had always welcomed research assignments.

"One day the light bulb went on for me," she recalls. She quit her job a few weeks before the annual PhD Project conference, turned down an offer for a highly prized job opening at another prominent corporation, and applied to Duke, where she had always dreamed of studying. Today she is a professor at North Carolina Central University, where she integrates the practical experiences of her sixteen corporate years into her teaching.

To succeed in earning a doctorate, Dr. Hunter-Rainey has learned, "You have to ask yourself why you are doing this. You have to know why; you have to be internally motivated. It can't be because you are fed up with corporate politics. You have to be engaged in it, and working with the people in your department."

A sense of humor also helps. Dr. Hunter-Rainey still enjoys a laugh as she recollects her young son's trenchant observation about her pursuit of the doctoral degree. "Mommy," Morgan said to her one day. "You've gone to college three times now. Aren't you listening to what they're saying?"

The dream continues...
*Dr. Hunter-Rainey was one of three recipients of the North
Carolina Central University Award for Teaching Excellence in
2008-09. Her NCCU School of Business students have also
recognized her work with the Students' Choice Graduate
Teacher of the Year in 2009-10, Students' Choice
Undergraduate Most Influential Faculty in 2008-09 and 2009-
10, plus Students' Choice Undergraduate Teacher of the Year in
2006-07. She is now an Associate Professor of Management at
Langston University. "To achieve balance I have mastered the
art of the strategic 'no' to protect my most valuable resource, my
time, to remain focused on my family and my career."*

An encounter in church

Dr. Michael DeVaughn
University of St. Thomas
Ph.D. University of Wisconsin, Madison, management

Michael DeVaughn, a human resources executive in banking, lived in the same town where he had attended college. He belonged to the same church as one of his former professors. One August day six years after DeVaughn graduated, the professor approached him in desperation. Teaching a popular course, he unexpectedly found himself needing two more teaching assistants for the fall. Was Michael interested?

DeVaughn agreed to try it. "After a year and a half, in which I was always coming home all frazzled from my job, my wife said, 'I see you so fired up from this little one hour a week in class—why don't you consider really doing it?' Within a month, I received The PhD Project's mailer. It felt as if the sun, moon, and earth had lined up. So I went for it."

Dr. DeVaughn takes pride in earning his doctorate from one recognized research institution and accepting a position in another, but his greatest satisfaction comes from "the interaction with the student—the charge I get out of seeing them try to soak up what I'm saying." The father of three young children, Dr. DeVaughn is also gratified that "I emerged with everything intact—marriage, kids. I struck a good balance all the way."

The dream continues...

In 2008, Dr. DeVaughn moved to a tenure-track position at the University of St. Thomas (Minneapolis, MN). He has published two book chapters, has a forthcoming article in a leading management journal, and has won a "best paper" award at the Academy of Management (2007). The Strategic Management Society recently awarded him a junior faculty research grant. Outside of the academy, he coaches his daughter's basketball team and his son and daughter's track and field team.

Committee decision

Dr. Lynette Wood
Winston-Salem State University
Ph.D. Indiana University, accounting

Accepted by nine universities that were bidding competitively for her, Dr. Lynette Wood put the difficult choice of which offer to accept into the hands of a committee. A family committee.

"My husband and children were fully involved in my search. Some schools were very prestigious, but the family said, 'No way,'" she recalls.

Dr. Wood took her husband and their two pre-teen children to several campuses, none of them near their Alabama home, for personal visits. Indiana University won out, and it also gained a new Master's student in journalism: Dr. Wood's husband.

A onetime consultant and entrepreneur, Dr. Wood had dropped out of college after one year for financial reasons. She returned to undergraduate studies at age twenty-nine on a full scholarship and went on to earn her Masters. By now she thoroughly understood both the value of higher education and the critical importance of timing in a career move. She had planned to delay pursuing her doctorate until the children were older. Her department chair encouraged her to accelerate the timetable, pointing out that, "there were good opportunities right now."

"I respond well to opportunity," she observes.

Fully committed as she was to the doctoral program, Dr. Wood had two even higher priorities in her life: her faith and her family. Throughout her Ph.D. studies, she remained an actively engaged mother—one who performed several hours of church volunteer work weekly in addition to her academic role.

"I would not make a choice that put career before children. I treated the doctoral program as a job," she explains. "Many mothers work. I was there for my children as a typical mother would be. When they were at school, so was I. When they went to bed, I went back to work. I just focused; I was more intense when at work."

Through her church, Dr. Wood ran community outreach and service programs, and participated in lay ministry activities, when not cramming the books or attending to her children.

"It took me a little longer, but I finished. I tried to have a fulfilling life. I didn't want to be so stressed out that I would be overwhelmed. It wasn't easy, but it was do-able."

Today at Virginia Tech University, Dr. Wood reports that her youngest child has finished college. On campus, this professor plays an active role in the lives of many current and former students, often meeting with them outside of class hours to mentor and advise. Sometimes a student's needs are more personal than academic. Through the years, Dr. Wood has demonstrated her caring for them by inviting groups of students to dine at her home regularly. Once during office hours, a student whose husband had left her as her mother was dying came by just to talk. Dr. Wood provided a sympathetic ear.

Not surprisingly, Dr. Wood places a high premium on active learning in the classroom. "I use a coach-team approach. I find out what they want to accomplish, and I help them accomplish it. I lecture very little in the classroom; I give students the opportunity to be interactive."

"It is so satisfying to know that I have been able to make a difference in students' lives, says Dr. Wood. "I've had students call me at home to say 'Happy New Year' and 'Happy Mother's Day.' That's special."

The dream continues...

Prior to Dr. Wood's arrival at her original university Virginia Tech, with African-Americans comprising 3% of the student body, did not have a chapter of the National Association of Black Accountants as chartering one is a rigorous, complex process. Dr. Wood took on the challenge and succeeded; 70% of the African-American accounting majors now belong. In addition to teaching, she is increasing her attention to campus-wide diversity recruiting issues, and continues to advise students on professional development. African-American students in many majors seek her out informally for guidance and support. Dr. Wood is now chair of the Department of Accounting & Management Information Systems at Winston-Salem State University.

Balancing

Dr. Maria Sanchez
Rider University
Ph.D. Drexel University, accounting

At dinnertime as a child, Maria Sanchez took it for granted that her mother and father would join her around the table virtually every evening to share the day's experiences. Most summers, one or both parents would be off, and the family would depart for lengthy, often exciting vacations.

Before long, the young girl realized that she had it better than most of her friends. And eventually she figured out why: her mom and dad were professors, her friends' parents worked in business.

Maria Sanchez never forgot the happy work-life balance her parents had achieved—or the satisfaction they derived from influencing students' minds. After several years with a Big Four accounting firm in which home was usually a hotel room somewhere, she too found herself yearning to make a lasting impact on the next generation. She decided to become a professor too.

"Being able to help students is something I knew I would really enjoy," she says. "And I do."

Flexibility and balance have a different meaning for her at this stage of life. These days, she can often be found running errands on a Tuesday morning, while Saturday might be swallowed up with research work or grading papers.

"I still work the same number of hours as I did," says Dr. Sanchez, "but with flexibility. I enjoy a work-life balance that comes with a career in academia."

All that, plus she gets to avoid rush hour on the busy roads around Philadelphia.

More importantly, she gets to influence students on career and academic decisions as she interacts with them in the classroom and in her office. "Several students in my auditing class told me they made the choice to enter public accounting based on my class," she reports.

But guiding young people to career choices is only the beginning. Students are often in the dark about how to conduct themselves on a job interview. "They'll come in and ask me how to handle interview questions, and while I do that, I also show them how to *ask* the right questions also."

One graduate student in accounting is even more indebted to Professor Sanchez. "He was in one of my courses, and I realized he was a very good candidate for an AICPA scholarship. He didn't even know they existed, and I showed him how to get one."

The student now has his Masters, and still sends Dr. Sanchez regular news about his career progress. He will soon be able to track hers too—her second research paper has been accepted for 2004 publication in one of her field's prominent journals.

The dream continues...

Dr. Sanchez has recorded several personal and professional milestones: marriage, motherhood, thirteen publications, tenure and promotion to Professor of Accounting at Rider University. She has been named to numerous fellowships and earned honors for her research, and she has spoken at PhD Project conferences. Dr. Sanchez is faculty advisor to the Rider University Beta Alpha Psi chapter and its Equestrian Club. She recently wrote a recommendation letter for the graduate student who received an AICPA scholarship and he is now applying to Ph.D. programs.

"If she can..."

Dr. Kimberly Dillon Grantham
University of Georgia
Ph.D. Duke University, marketing

As an undergraduate at the University of Virginia, Kimberly Dillon Grantham admits she "had no clue what a Ph.D. was—or what I could do with it."

What she did know was that attending her favorite professor's class ignited an unexpected spark for her. "I liked his job, and I wanted to know what I had to do to get a job like his," she recalls. "I didn't even know anything about the research part; I just saw the teaching part, and I wanted to put myself in his shoes."

It didn't take long to fill in the parts she didn't know, and after attending the first PhD Project conference in 1994, Dr. Grantham enrolled in Duke's doctoral program. By the time she was completing her dissertation to earn her doctorate from Duke, Dr. Grantham was already teaching at a college in Georgia. "My husband was extremely supportive and encouraging during this very challenging time," she says. "I believe that this support, the support of my dissertation committee, along with a strong faith in God's divine plan, is very important."

Starting her professorial career at Clark Atlanta University, she saw many students sitting before her who were, as she once was, unaware that becoming a professor is a viable career option. "The most rewarding part of what I did at Clark Atlanta was letting other African-American and minority students realize that attaining a Ph.D. is something they can do. They would see me, they would think; 'If she can do it, I can do it.'"

Dr. Grantham continues to build her career now at the University of Georgia. Her greatest accomplishment, she believes, is "getting married happily during my studies in a dual career marriage, having a child, growing spiritually, achieving a balance in my life, and then showing my students that it can be done. It takes sacrifice, but it can be done—and it is all worth the effort.

"Now I am blessed to live and work in the same city, Athens, Georgia. This is the first time ever that I have not had to commute at least one and a half hours to get to work. We can better manage the responsibilities of raising our son, and our careers, without the long commute."

The dream continues...
At the University of Georgia, Dr. Grantham teaches both large lecture undergraduate classes and smaller upper level discussion oriented courses. She values her role as mentor to students and reports, "It has been extremely rewarding to see students whom I mentor excel in corporations by applying what they've learned from UGA and by making innovative contributions." Dr. Grantham and her husband share their professional home at UGA, and they balance dual careers in academia while raising two young sons and a daughter. Dr. Grantham continues to enjoy her career and was promoted to Senior Lecturer at UGA in 2010. "I love teaching and my Senior Lecturer position affords me the opportunity to excel in this professional area while I achieve balance with my marriage-parent-work roles," she says.

Living the dream

138

Chosen

Dr. Laquita Blockson
Rutgers Business School
Ph.D. University of Pittsburgh, management

"I'm a role model as soon as I walk into the classroom," says Professor Laquita Blockson. "When I enter the room and say 'I'm Professor Blockson,' I can hear them say, 'Whoa!'"

Dr. Blockson first began contemplating a career as an educator when she was an undergraduate at Florida A&M University. It was there she realized that academics came in all colors. "I had never seen so many Black faculty before."

But a corporate career beckoned, and she became a real estate manager for Taco Bell. The dream of teaching simmered on a back burner, and eventually, she attended a PhD Project conference. There, her life changed in an instant. "It all hit home. I realized you were chosen. This is your profession."

"As an undergraduate, you memorize concepts. As a graduate student, you apply them. And as a doctoral student, you get to question the concepts and come up with new ones. Now, I want to be able to give back to others what my faculty once gave to me."

One student who encountered Dr. Blockson was struggling to balance a full time job, uphold family responsibilities, complete her studies, and pursue admission to graduate school.

"She was Jamaican, and she was very happy to see a Black woman teaching, so she sought me out. I mentored her far beyond professional development. We worked on how to apply, how to interview, and which programs fit her best. She was able to graduate and get accepted by one of her choice schools."

The dream continues...

Dr. Blockson is now an Associate Professor at Rutgers Business School, where she continues to be a role model and mentor for African-American undergraduates. Before joining Rutgers, she was an Assistant Professor at Saint Leo University where she created and introduced a course on minority entrepreneurship and collaborated with two other PhD Project professors – Dr. Jeffrey Robinson and Dr. Sammie Robinson -- on a Kauffman Foundation-funded study of African American women entrepreneurs. She is the co-recipient (along with fellow PhD Project professor Dr. Ian Williamson) of the 2005 Academy of Management's Mentoring Best Practices Award, for her leadership in forming the Management Faculty of Color Association. In addition to her research, teaching and mentoring, Dr. Blockson finds time to coach nonprofit and development organizations within underserved communities. For her work, she was noted in 2009 by Diverse Magazine as one of its "Emerging Scholars."

Influences

Dr. Gail Dawson
University of Tennessee, Chattanooga
Ph.D. University of South Florida, management

Growing up, Gail Dawson had never considered that there might be African-Americans teaching college. It was not until she enrolled at Florida A&M as an undergraduate that she learned otherwise. There, she encountered several faculty members who would influence her life. Starting a business career and earning an MBA, she recalls, "I was always looking for something where I could make more of a difference. Then, I heard about The PhD Project and I thought, 'That's it.' I had had role models at Florida A&M, and I wanted to be one for others."

As a professor, she has counseled and mentored numerous students, including some "who seemed to be a little lost. I advise students on how to get through college, and I help prepare them for what is coming next. Students have told me they never took school seriously until my class." One student she guided was accepted to graduate school, winning a scholarship from the National Society of Hispanic MBAs. "I couldn't be more proud," she says, "having seen this young man grow and mature over the past three and one-half years."

For two years, the only African-American on the business school faculty, she put her school in touch with other PhD Project participants. Two of them were hired. "We tripled the number," Dr. Dawson says proudly.

The dream continues...

Dr. Dawson earned tenure and is now Associate Professor of Management. She received honors for faculty achievement and minority leadership at her university, and has published many articles, focusing most frequently on corporate diversity issues. She published her first poetry book—Straight to the Point: Poems for Real People, comprised of poems that "cover a variety of real world topics." She also serves on the boards of several nonprofit organizations.

Notes in a drawer

Dr. Ashleigh Rosette
Duke University
Ph.D. Northwestern University, management

Dr. Ashleigh Rosette keeps the handwritten notes and e-mails stuffed into a drawer at home, and there are now many of them. Typically, they start by recounting how much the writer enjoyed taking Dr. Rosette's class. Often, they go on to reveal that the author is now considering—or pursuing—a career in management because of Dr. Rosette's influence.

She saves each note as a silent reminder of the reason she became an educator.

In addition to fulfilling her responsibilities as a doctoral candidate and now a professor, Dr. Rosette has carved out time to mentor and teach high school students, through programs like LEAD, about the benefits of a career in business. It is these young people whose personal messages fill her drawer.

When a faculty member in her MBA school first raised the idea of becoming a professor, "I said no, I've never considered a career in academia." But after several years of "working seventy-hour weeks with little control over daily activities" in public accounting, she reconsidered. "Now," says Dr. Rosette, "I may still work seventy hours a week, but I control what I do each day."

Poised to leave the business world and enter a doctoral program, Dr. Rosette paused to consider her husband's circumstances. An attorney, he had just passed the bar exam in their home state of Texas a year earlier. Moving to Northwestern University in Chicago would require him not only to find a new job, but also to take the bar exam of another state. The couple talked it over, and "his support was unconditional."

The decision made, Dr. Rosette gained acceptance, and on the very day she submitted her resignation to her accounting firm, her husband received a job offer in Chicago.

Dr. Rosette values most, as a professor, "the flexible schedule of an educator and the freedom to pursue research topics such as discrimination and structural inequities. These topics are not at the forefront of management research, but are important and need to be considered."

"In teaching," she adds, "my goal is to challenge every person who steps through that door."

The dream continues...

Dr. Rosette is now Associate Professor at Duke University. She has numerous teaching and research honors, with six publications to date on a range of topics, many diversity-related, and eighteen presentations including several with fellow PhD Project participant Patricia Hewlin. She is Faculty Advisor to the PhD Project Management Doctoral Student Association, co-chaired the 2005 Management Faculty of Color Annual Conference, taught business study-bound high school students in LEAD, and was a Fellow in the Center for the Study of Race, Ethnicity, and Gender in Social Sciences.

144

Old friends

Dr. Dawn Pearcy
Eastern Michigan University
Ph.D. Florida State University, marketing

Dawn Pearcy, contemplating an exit from corporate life after several years at a major automaker, sat in the audience as a video program opened the 1997 PhD Project conference. Huge images of the then-small handful of newly minted minority professors loomed over the crowded auditorium.

"Oh my God," she whispered as one face flickered on the giant screen. "That woman looks like Gail."

The woman on the screen was indeed Gail Ayala Taylor—Dawn Pearcy's first childhood friend, whom she had not seen in more than a decade. Dr. Taylor had just become a business professor.

Dawn Pearcy had walked into the conference planning to leave her job and become a business professor. But when she saw that the girl who had been her best friend and neighbor at age five had chosen exactly the same career path, she knew it was a done deal.

On that extraordinary day in 1997, Dr. Taylor was also in the audience. Dawn Pearcy located her in the first break.

The two women renewed their friendship on the spot, but something equally significant occurred—from that moment on, Dr. Taylor became her childhood buddy's unofficial and ever-present guide and mentor through the daunting process of getting accepted to a doctoral program.

"Her guidance was instrumental throughout the entire program," says Dr. Pearcy. "When I needed help, she basically cleared her schedule for me."

In time, the girls who once played with dolls in preschool together would end up getting their business doctorates at the same institution—Florida State University.

Dr. Pearcy is now on faculty at Eastern Michigan University, where she has begun to fulfill her goal of "being more impactful."

In addition to teaching, she has already been published three times, and has presented eight conference papers.

The dream continues...

Dr. Pearcy was granted tenure and promoted to Associate Professor in 2007. Her research has been published in numerous journals and conference proceedings. She started a new stream of research on environmental sustainability and fair trade, an area that not only excited her but enabled her to co-author a paper with her sister Michelle. It was presented at an international conference in Botswana. Dr. Pearcy said, "I remain grateful to my first friend, Dr. Gail Ayala Taylor, for all her support during my career journey in academe. I am most grateful for her friendship, which has endured time, distance, and busy schedules. We'll remain friends forever."

The PhD Project reports, with sadness, that Dr. Pearcy passed away in January, 2015.

Eleventh hour challenge

Dr. Nicole Thorne Jenkins
University of Kentucky
Ph.D. University of Iowa, accounting

Professor Nicole Thorne Jenkins doesn't just help her students write their own success stories. She then puts them to work—for her.

Dr. Jenkins invested her own time, energy, and commitment into a student who was retaking the introductory accounting course after failing it with another instructor. "I encouraged her when she was discouraged. She came to my office for support, and we worked together," says Dr. Jenkins. "I have a different presentation to the course work, and that plus the support seemed to make a difference."

The struggling student earned an A, decided to dual-major in accounting, and is now Dr. Jenkins's research assistant.

Overcoming obstacles is something that Nicole Jenkins can preach, because she's practiced it. As a doctoral student, she had to scrap her entire Ph.D. dissertation nearly at the eleventh hour, when another scholar published a paper on the same topic. So she dusted herself off, stayed on for another year, and produced an all new dissertation.

Originally an accountant with a prominent multinational firm, Dr. Jenkins developed the urge to teach while tutoring engineers in calculus as an undergraduate. But she deferred the dream for several years in order to gain valuable experience in business. As a professor, she proselytizes for the accounting profession. "I enjoy drawing students in and showing them how accounting affects their lives even if they are not accountants. I show them what they can do with a degree in accounting, and the benefits of minoring in it. And I show them accounting is not as hard as they think it is!"

Many of Dr. Jenkins's students come to her at semester's end and tell her their dread of accounting melted away with her case-oriented, team-learning style of teaching. Some of them even sign up for the next course.

All of which helps to explain why Dr. Jenkins won two teaching awards while earning her doctorate at the University of Iowa.

The dream continues...

Now on faculty at the University of Kentucky, Dr. Jenkins has become an acknowledged expert on the topic of the effects of accounting restatements and share repurchases. She has published articles in The Journal of Accounting and Economics, Review of Accounting Studies, and The Accounting Review. The student she supported and developed into a research assistant is now herself a professor.

"Dr. Double"

Dr. Alisha Malloy
North Carolina Central University
Ph.D. Georgia State University, information systems

As early as age sixteen in her hometown of Kansas City, Missouri, Alisha Malloy knew she wanted to get her Ph. D. She discovered her desire to teach when she taught a computer class at her high school. She attended the U.S. Naval Academy and then served as a Naval Officer, holding positions in naval cryptology and war gaming. During her time in the Navy, she obtained a Masters in Engineering Management while raising two small children.

Once out of the Navy, Dr. Malloy entered the corporate world as a network and business analyst for Sprint. One day while at a friend's house thumbing through *Black Enterprise* magazine, she saw an ad for The PhD Project and decided to apply for the program's annual conference. Her children were ages three and six at the time. She recalls, "When I attended the annual conference and walked into that auditorium, I knew there was no turning back. I thought, 'This is what I was meant to be doing with my life.'" She finished her program in less than four years.

Upon completing, Dr. Malloy was crowned "Dr. Double." She had become the five hundred and eighty-eighth doctorally-qualified minority business professor in the United States, thus doubling the number of minority business professors from the two hundred and ninety-four who existed when The PhD Project began in 1994. Due to her extensive corporate background, Dr. Malloy says, "When students come to me seeking advice, I am equipped to guide them through their career decisions." She has helped countless students find the job for which they are best suited. Dr. Malloy teaches her students, "You must know the *process* before you can understand the *language*." One of Dr. Malloy's favorite quotes is: "No one rises to low expectations." Her next goal is to start a program to help bring technology to minorities through community service.

The dream continues...

Dr. Malloy is now an Associate Professor at North Carolina Central University (NCCU). Since 2004, she has received research grants and awards totaling approximately $1.5 million from the National Science Foundation, Cisco Systems, and the state of Alabama, among others. The Southern Regional Education Board (SREB) named her Faculty Mentor of the Year in 2006. She has published four articles and presented or published papers at many conferences. Dr. Malloy has served as a faculty mentor and presenter for The PhD Project Information Systems Doctoral Students Association, and one of the doctoral students she helped, Dr. Belinda Shipps, went on to become The PhD Project's Dr. Triple in 2008. Dr. Malloy continues her goal to bring technology to minorities through community service through the use of IBM Faculty Awards for Cloud Computing which provide access to Science, Technology, Engineering, and Mathematics (STEM) software applications for K-12 and community organizations using NCCU's Virtual Computing Lab. These initiatives allow the participants to use the software applications through virtual machines inside and outside the classroom.

Two a.m. phone call

Dr. Yancy Edwards
Sogang University
Ph.D. Ohio State University, business administration

Yancy Edwards knew when he began his Ph.D. studies that he'd soon be working into the early morning hours frequently. What he didn't anticipate was the 2:00 a.m. phone calls from an undergraduate struggling to make it through the college experience.

"I tutored many students, and my undergraduates have always come to me for advice, but this one was working full time while going for his bachelor's degree. He wanted to drop some courses.

"I encouraged him to get through it. He'd call me at 2:00 a.m., and I kept him motivated. He often said, 'If it wasn't for you, I wouldn't have made it.'"

All the while, the rigorous life of a doctoral student was posing its own challenges for Dr. Edwards. And, he says, "If it wasn't for The PhD Project, I wouldn't have been where I am now, either."

Where he is now is at Sogang University in Seoul, South Korea.

The dream continues...

Dr. Edwards' research involves building models that are more insightful and predictive of consumer behavior. These insights are used to develop and improve product development, promotion, market segmentation, and target marketing activities. He has published three articles, presented at six conferences, and has several works of research now in progress.

Moment of truth

Dr. Veronda Willis
University of Texas at Tyler
Ph.D. University of Colorado, accounting

"It's a paper she can't finish, or else she's on overload from juggling her job and school," thought newly-appointed accounting professor Dr. Veronda Willis when the young Hispanic woman hesitantly requested a private conference after class.

But Dr. Willis was about to hear a very different story—one that would demand of her, in this first semester on faculty at the University of Texas, San Antonio, something so extraordinary that a professor could go an entire career without ever facing it.

Speaking slowly and carefully at first, the student sketched out a disturbing tale. Working in her first accounting job, she had uncovered unmistakable evidence of serious financial fraud in her organization. The evidence pointed clearly to a culprit. It was her boss.

Confused, scared, and unsure of what to do—but keenly aware of the perilously high stakes for everyone—the woman had reached out to the one person she believed she could trust and rely on: her accounting professor, Dr. Willis.

For Dr. Willis, it was a moment of truth. Having enjoyed a successful career in accounting, first at a global firm and then in a major corporation, she had finally succumbed, some six years earlier, to the nagging urge to become a professor. Having come to cherish the assignment of training new employees for her employer, she had realized that as much as she loved accounting, the influence she could exert on the profession was still limited by the number of hours she could work. But by becoming a professor, she knew, her influence could be virtually limitless. She could, as she phrased it later, "be an influencer."

Dr. Willis's last employer had been Enron, and that company's dissolution, after she had left her well-paying position, sold her home, and moved from Houston to Boulder to earn a doctorate, left a deep impression. In every class she taught, first as a teaching assistant and now as a professor, she had stressed ethics, by developing hypothetical situations for her students to work through.

Now that focus on ethics had led a student to step forward bravely with exactly the kind of situation that Dr. Willis had been trying to prepare her students to face. She had just one chance to get it right, as the woman sat there waiting for guidance.

The student had turned to the right source for help. First, Dr. Willis calmed the woman, assuring her that the law would afford her full protection for doing the right thing. Then, she advised her student on the next course of action.

The student followed Dr. Willis's advice. She diplomatically approached her supervisor to confirm that she had indeed interpreted the facts correctly. Then she summoned her courage and went over her head, to tell senior-level management. The Board of Directors soon stepped in. An investigation unfolded, and when it was over, her boss was terminated. Throughout the semester, Dr. Willis continued to advise and support her student.

When it was all over, the student wrote in an e-mail, "I consider myself a very lucky student for having you as one of my professors. You've made me feel like your students are important to you."

"When I work on ethics issues with my students in class," says Dr. Willis, "it's not like I can tell them what to do. But I can prepare them for situations they might face. In accounting, there are areas where there is not always a clear

154

'right' or 'wrong' answer. You have to make choices, and you want them to be the right choices."

"And as a professor," she adds, "you want people to know when it is time to make a choice—and when it is time to speak out."

The dream continues...

Dr. Willis is now an Assistant Professor of Accounting at the University of Texas at Tyler (her hometown) and continues to influence and mentor students regularly, if not in the dramatic manner of her whistle-blower student, who eventually left her position voluntarily and is now successfully employed elsewhere. Dr. Willis presents her research at numerous conferences and she has been published in various accounting journals such as Accounting, Organizations & Society, Issues in Accounting Education and Oil & Gas Quarterly. She conducts financial reporting research in the deregulated electric utility industry and in accounting education. She currently serves as the faculty advisor for the UT-Tyler Beta Alpha Psi Chapter and is Associate Director of the Hibbs Institute for Business & Economic Research. In 2010, she received the Outstanding College of Business Faculty Award from the UT-Tyler Alpha Chi Chapter.

Following his heart

Dr. J. Alberto Espinosa
American University
Ph.D. Carnegie Mellon University, information systems

In 1983, Dr. J. Alberto Espinosa decided to get his Ph.D. in finance from Texas Tech University. After a year in the program, he realized that he was more interested in information systems than in finance.

Because Ph.D. studies require such a strong time commitment, he decided to enter the work force to gain more practical experience in IS. He worked in a number of capacities at international nonprofit organizations, including Director of Management Information Systems and Chief Financial Officer.

However, his brief experience in a Ph.D. program had left him with a taste for research and teaching that never went away.

After a few years as a senior manager, Dr. Espinosa decided it was time to return to school and do what his heart was telling him to do. "I really love research and teaching. I could not get it out of my system, so I knew I had to return to school and finish my studies."

So, fourteen years after beginning his doctoral work, he went back to school to complete his Ph.D., but this time in information systems.

156

He joined The PhD Project's Doctoral Students Association. "I found an excellent peer group and outstanding faculty in The PhD Project, eager to provide us with guidance and mentorship. These were key to helping me define my career goals, prepare for the job market, and make the correct placement decisions," he says.

Dr. Espinosa brings a lot of his work experience into the classroom and has guided many students to career choices in IS. He also won a student teaching award from Carnegie Mellon. "A few of my students tell me they changed career paths to IS because of what they learned in my class. That makes it all worthwhile."

The dream continues...

Dr. Espinosa was granted tenure and promoted to Associate Professor in 2008 and since then has been promoted to Full Professor. His work has been published in leading journals including: Management Science; Organization Science; the Journal of Management Information Systems; Communications of the ACM; Information, Technology, and People; and Software Process: Improvement and Practice. His work has also been published in leading academic conference proceedings, and he is a frequent presenter in those conferences.

Instant family

Dr. Richard Jones
Hofstra University
Ph.D. Rutgers University, accounting

Dr. Jones started on the road to his Ph.D. in 1993, after leaving his controller position at a prominent bank. At the first PhD Project Accounting Doctoral Students Association (DSA) meeting the next year, "I met so many people with the same experiences as me, it was like instant family. It was definitely a driving force to help me get through my doctoral process."

In 1997, he received an offer to teach from Hofstra University and, wanting to start making an impact while writing his dissertation, he accepted. "Working there and attending the DSA meetings each year kept me on track. I knew I would eventually finish my Ph.D.— it was just a matter of time."

Dr. Jones finds that his freshman and sophomore students ask him about accounting as a major, and his juniors and seniors want to know about his work experience. "It's really great to be able to mentor and guide students of all ages into the right academic and career choices," he says. "I love my job!"

Students at Hofstra University elected Dr. Jones "Distinguished Teacher of the Year" in 2001, and the faculty elected him the recipient of the business school's Outstanding

Teacher of the Year award. He is the only full time African-American accounting professor at Hofstra's school of business.

The dream continues...

Now an Associate Professor at Hofstra, Dr. Jones has been published in several journals. He teaches in a university summer residency program that exposes high school juniors to career opportunities in accounting. During a recent sabbatical, he worked with a major accounting firm to design and present a professional education course on international accounting standards.

The best time

Dr. Diana Robinson
North Carolina A&T University
Ph.D. Oklahoma State University, accounting

Dr. Diana Robinson taught college without a Ph.D. degree for longer than most minority business school professors have taught with one.

For ten years, she served as a non-tenure track instructor at several colleges including North Carolina A&T before finally deciding that she needed to realize her full promise and become a tenured professor.

"I had not gotten into the research part of being a professor, and I needed to challenge my brain," she remembers. She attended a PhD Project conference where she was "blown away," as she realized that "I wanted to see what research is all about, and you need to earn the degree to be able to do all the things you want to do."

Although twelve years had elapsed since she had last been a student, Dr. Robinson knew the timing was right for her. "There is a certain level of maturity you need to get through the day-to-day challenges of a Ph.D. program. I was at the right stage in my life; it was the best time for me."

Teaching college had been part of Dr. Robinson's life since childhood. Her parents were professors and, even as a young girl, Dr. Robinson noticed and appreciated that she saw her mom and dad around home more than her friends saw theirs. Upon graduating college, she started teaching business math at a community college while working days in corporate jobs. Her employers groomed her for management, but her department chair continually urged her to teach full time. "I just enjoyed teaching too much not to do it full time," she says.

After earning her doctorate, Dr. Robinson returned to a tenure-track position at North Carolina A&T, the last college where she taught. Dr. Robinson is now not only a tenured, full and fulfilled professor, but she is one of the PhD Project's leading unofficial "recruiters." By her own estimate, she has persuaded at least three of her students to enter doctoral programs and become business professors.

The dream continues...

Following her desire to do research, Dr. Robinson has recently been published in CPA Journal and other publications, and is doing research on topics related to diversity and accounting, with additional publications scheduled. She mentors students who are considering careers in accounting, and continues to recruit future professors to The PhD Project. "Most of the time we guide our students to corporate or public accounting careers. Many of them have no idea they could consider a career in academia."

Floored

Dr. Karen Nunez
Elon University
Ph.D. University of Oklahoma, accounting

Before becoming a professor, Dr. Nunez worked in the corporate world for Pepsico, Pillsbury, and KPMG, LLP. She brings much of her work force experience into her teaching. "I always find that students learn more and their learning experience is enhanced by my real-world examples," she says.

After teaching for five years without a Ph.D. at Loyola University of Chicago and the University of Baltimore, Dr. Nunez heard about The PhD Project through her dean at Baltimore. She decided to attend the very first PhD Project Conference. "I was floored. I could not believe how much I learned in forty-eight hours! It was an entire education unto itself. I was immediately hooked," she recalls.

Being chosen "Outstanding Graduate Teaching Assistant" at the University of Oklahoma was just one of the many milestones in Dr. Karen Nunez's doctoral process. She also received a Graduate Student Research Award and was hired to teach at North Carolina State even before she defended her dissertation.

The dream continues...

Dr. Nunez is now on the faculty at Elon University. She was honored in the 2006 Lybrand Awards Manuscript Competition of the Institute of Management Accountants. She received a Best Paper award from the 2004 International Applied Business Research Conference for her manuscript on utility deregulation, "Electric Utilities: Stranded Costs vs. Stranded Benefits," which is among more than twenty-five publications and presentations to her credit. For two years she held a funded Enterprise Risk Management Faculty Fellowship at North Carolina State University.

They saw it in him

Dr. Andy Garcia
Bowling Green State University
Ph.D. Texas Tech, accounting

Ex-Marine, now Colorado State University freshman, Andy Garcia looked in the mirror and saw a student. But when the academicians looked at him, they saw a future peer.

"I was sitting in my counselor's office, making the case for why I should be allowed to take an introductory accounting course out of sequence. I pulled out a grid chart where I had mapped out the course sequence I wanted to take for my whole four years," Dr. Garcia recalls.

"Who are you, and where did you come from?" the counselor asked the freshman. She then stunned him by interrupting the discussion and walking him down the hall to meet the dean of the business school.

Something in the ex-Marine's demeanor and his rigorous, self-disciplined approach to his education resonated in the counselor and the dean. On the spot, they urged him to enroll in the Minority Summer Institute, a 1990s nationwide effort to encourage undergraduates to become business professors. "At that point, I hadn't even considered becoming a professor. They saw it in me before I saw it myself," Dr. Garcia admits.

The accounting student attended the program, viewing it initially as simply a paid opportunity to acquire knowledge and earn academic credit. But upon becoming immersed in the summer program, he began hearing about "the psychic rewards of becoming a professor."

Listening to professors describe how they had influenced the lives of countless students, mentoring them, and guiding their career choices, Dr. Garcia made a sudden realization: this was exactly what the dean and the counselor at Colorado State had done for him. It was why he was sitting in that very classroom.

"What they were describing had just happened to me, and I thought, 'Wouldn't it be nice to be able to give something back like that,'" he says. Then and there, he decided to become a professor.

Observing his own teachers closely, Dr. Garcia identified the factors that defined the best of them. As systematically as he had charted out his undergraduate course sequence, he set out to emulate the career track that seemed to mark the most effective professors. The path, he determined, would include earning an MBA and CPA, and several years in business—with a healthy sprinkling of overseas experience. Methodically, he also plotted out a financial plan to establish a financial cushion for four or five years of doctoral studies.

The plan would unfold just as he envisioned it: four years at a Fortune 500 company and a Big Four accounting firm, with extensive service in Latin America and Asia; a fortuitous introduction at the PhD Project conference to the Texas Tech professor who would become his dissertation committee chairman; late-night moonlighting sessions in hotels in Caracas or Bogotá to prep for the GMAT and line up references; and smooth admission into Texas Tech.

When the wheels fell off midway through his doctoral program, it was nothing that Andy Garcia could have anticipated or prevented.

Not once, but twice during his coursework at Texas Tech, departmental changes led to curriculum overhauls that lengthened the list of required courses. Having prepared and budgeted meticulously to afford four low-income years of doctoral studies, Dr. Garcia now faced seven years.

As the temptation to quit swelled within him, Dr. Garcia reached out to other doctoral students around the nation whom he had met through the PhD Project. He was surprised to hear tales of serious setbacks from many of them—"and many of those were more challenging than what I was facing."

"So I looked myself in the mirror and said, 'Get yourself together. You can do it.'" The accounting student reassessed his personal balance sheet. Selling some of his belongings on eBay and moving into a smaller apartment, he made the financial adjustments that pulled him through.

Today, Professor Andy Garcia reports he is "very happy—I really, really like what I do. When I was in business, I was just getting up and going to work. Now, I wake up looking forward to it."

The dream continues...

Dr. Garcia is a tenured associate professor with ten articles published with two more accepted and forthcoming. He recently won a "Best Paper Award" at the AAA conference (2011) and has presented, moderated, and been a discussant at numerous other conferences. He is faculty advisor to Beta Alpha Psi and has served on Bowling Green's faculty senate, curriculum committee, graduate advisory council, and scholarships and awards committee. He has also been an outside reviewer on two Ph.D. committees.

<u>The PhD Project</u>

Funding provided by:

KPMG Foundation

Graduate Management Admission Council

Citi Foundation

AACSB International

300+ Participating Universities

AICPA Foundation

DiversityInc

Dixon Hughes Goodman LLP

Rockwell Collins

Wal-Mart Stores. Inc.

American Marketing Association

John Deere Foundation

CIGNA

Edison International (on behalf of the Cal State University System)

Lincoln Financial Group

Aerotek & TEKsystems (operating companies of Allegis Group)

American Accounting Association

The Hershey Company

Academy of Management

NASBA

Ocwen Financial Corporation

Thrivent Financial

Founders

Alphabetical Index

Alphabetical Index cont...

Alphabetical Index cont...

Index by Discipline

Index by Discipline cont...

Index of Institutions, Organizations and Publications

Index of Institutions, Organizations and Publications cont...

Index of Institutions, Organizations and Publications cont...

Index of Institutions, Organizations and Publications cont...

Index of Institutions, Organizations and Publications cont...

Index of Institutions, Organizations and Publications cont...

To Learn More, Visit:
www.phdproject.org